Listening With

The Heart

Dee Martin

Listening With The Heart

Copyright © 2021 by Dee Martin

All rights reserved.

Published by Red Penguin Books

Bellerose Village, New York

Library of Congress Control Number: 2021910353

ISBN

Print 978-1-63777-064-1

Digital 978-1-63777-065-8

The publisher and the author are providing this book and its contents and make no representations or warranties of any kind with respect to this book or its contents. The publisher and the author disclaim all such representations and warranties, including but not limited to warranties of healthcare for a particular purpose. In addition, the publisher and the author assume no responsibility for errors, inaccuracies, omissions, or any other inconsistencies herein.

The author claims that all contents of this book are not to be read as "the truth" or in any way replace, exalt or diminish any already existent psychological disciplines and therapies as well as any and all books written on the subject of parenting. This book is to be read as the author's personal account and discovery of her experience of parenting and is meant to awaken the reader to reflect on and seek out any disciplines that may further the reader's discovery and expansion of self in the area of parenting. Any references to people in this book represent a composite of the author's personal and professional experiences over many decades and are not meant to refer to any particular persons living or dead.

I dedicate this book to my **daughter**, *whose birth gave me purpose, courage and determination to rise above and transcend my childhood wounds.*

And To

My **son,** *whose birth ignited my love for being a mother and opened my heart to listen to him and to all human beings with love and compassion.*

I also dedicate this book to the mothers and fathers who have had or will have the courage to bring life into the world, as well as to the incredible human beings who parented the children of those who gave birth but were not able to raise them.

We are interdependent even when we think we are separate or alone. My desire is that we listen to each unique life in our future generations and raise all our children UP!

In Praise of Dee Martin

When we went to see Dee Martin for couples therapy we were at the brink of divorce. Our two adolescent kids were having issues with depression. We were arguing every day. As a result of our work with Ms Martin we are communicating and solving our issues peacefully. We have created family meetings with our kids. We discuss issues calmly and we are closer and more loving.

~The Keenan family

Listening With The Heart, such an appropriate title! That is who Dee Martin is as a psychologist and psychotherapist. She listens and sees who people are with a depth of heart. I have been in counseling with her and I am able to really listen to people. I can connect to their world and it has been an incredible gift to me and my family.

~M Burger

Dee Martin creates a space of inspiration, empowerment and love. Working with her allowed me to dismantle the barriers that stopped me in many areas of my life. Dee's deep and lasting transformative work revolutionized my relationship to myself and those I love. I now accept and embrace all of me: experiencing myself and my life with complete freedom, delight and open-heartedness. In my family, I see my husband and children for who they truly are and easily connect and listen to them with love.

~ Helen Orchard

Acknowledgements

I would like to acknowledge the following people who have had a significant input in my life as well as in writing this book:

- My grandmother Josefa and my grandfather Alfio, who gave me unconditional love and showed me care in my first 7 years of life.

- My mother Delia and my father Roberto, for giving me life and so many talents.

- All of my clients, who over 38 years gifted me with their trust, their pains and their joys as they broke out of their past and into new ways to fully live life.

- Helen Orchard, whose grace, kindness, and support not only assisted me with the cover of this book, but also with the editing. I also want to acknowledge Helen's courage to share deeply her journey of parenting her son Oliver.

- Michelle Gay, dear friend and generous spirit, who led me to my editor, Stephanie Larkin.

- Werner Erhard, whose transformational work has been an undeniable source of my freedom to be and create my life.

- Landmark Worldwide and its programs and each seminar leader who played a part in empowering me to live a life of my own design.

- A special thanks to my friend and coach, Steve Conenna, who through a conversation inspired me to complete this book.

- Jorge Alfano, my friend, for his inspiration, wisdom and music that he so generously gifted me to use in my book release.

- Finally, I thank all the human beings who have contributed to me and opened my eyes to the depth of the human spirit.

Contents

Prologue

Listening With The Heart is a book dedicated to the expansion of the parent as a conscious instrument to raising their children. This book is not a how-to book, for there are many books written which can give guidelines as to how to deal with particular childhood issues. Becoming a conscious parent vs. being an unconscious parent refers to a way of being fully present, aware, focused, and tuned into each particular child with the openness of discovering who this unique being is. Instead of merely following a set of guidelines, which we learned or were set up by our culture to condition the child into the society, we must not overlook, but emphasize the most important ingredient in raising our children, which is that they are here as a pure vessel of love. In order for us to welcome the gift of each child, we must empty ourselves of preconceived ideas of how this child "should" be, could be, or will be. We must have an "open heart" and a keen awareness to listen beyond words to capture the beauty and the potential that each child brings at birth.

When my daughter was born, I was neither present nor even aware of what her soul brought to me. As I was still a child myself, I focused on her survival (food, clothing, education, etc.), which are all important ingredients for raising a healthy child. I missed out on what her soul and beauty brought to me, and, in turn, I was not able to give her the valuable feedback that a conscious listening of her would have provided. The ultimate gift as we co-create with each child as we are listening with an open heart is that parent and child experience their mutual love and the task of parenting becomes one of ease, joy, and fulfillment.

When I brought my son into the world, I was much older. I had been looking profoundly at the ways that I had been parented and I was well on my journey from being an unconscious to a conscious parent. My heart was open to accepting every task, every challenge, every moment with a sense of wonder, curiosity, and appreciation for this "new being" that I called my son and all that he brought to my life. We engaged in a mutual discovery and we co-created each other. He taught me how to open myself to love and my love gave him his wings to find his way in this world.

I hope that you can be inspired and moved by my personal journey and what I teach and provide for parents who want to become *Listeners Of The Heart.*

Overview and Philosophy

Listening With The Heart is the result of a shift in who the parent is Being. The parent has an awakening in being present and listening for who their child is. In the process of discovering who the child is by being present to the unique characteristics of the child, the parent is able to empower the child to develop his/her potential without repressing the Self. In other words, to maintain the child whole and complete during all stages of his or her development.

In *Listening With The Heart*, we as parents do not focus on what are good parenting skills. We become conscious of how being present with your child gives way to an experience of mutual growth and collaboration between parent and child. I do not tell you what to do but have you discover and access this potential of being a parent that resides within you. I also discuss tapping into your intuitive intelligence, which is undervalued in our society. This intuitive intelligence, when it is nurtured, allows you to know organically what is needed to comfort, support, and motivate your child.

Each child comes with a purity that can heal us. They come to earth to show us that love is the gift that our emphasis on survival has obscured. Their innocence is the gift that the veil of fear has denied us. Co-creating and listening with a firm but open heart will re-open the pathway to remove alienation and separation from our journey through parenting.

Communication with your child is fundamental for him or her to grow physically, emotionally, mentally, and spiritually into his or her uniqueness. As parents, we are child developers. Our parenting skills need to assure us that we are not only adjusting our children into the social structure, but we are taking care of their souls. I come from the view that we are all born whole and complete. That is, we are born, and there are no defects. The defects are interpreted by our human view of what we have considered to be acceptable. While many forms of nature exist, we as humans also are distinct and unique exactly as we are. The creator does not make mistakes. Children are born with "batteries included." They are coded with whatever they need to be in this world. Some human beings that we call special needs are just born with a uniqueness that our society does not accept as complete or whole.

As child developers, our job is to discover, uncover, and empower their unique potential without breaking their wills. While we may want compliance and collaboration, we are not to motivate this through fear, but rather through love. This love is a way of being that transmits to the child that you are OK, exactly as you are, even when the behavior may not be acceptable. There is a distinct difference between addressing "who the child is" vs. "unacceptable behavior." For generations, these have been collapsed. We are then not to make our children into our likeness, but to raise our children up by empowering them to become exactly the way that they are here "to be" while our role is to show them the ways of the world so they can make their way and make a difference to the social structure.

To become a conscious parent, or a *Listener Of The Heart*, you must be willing to do the following:

Number One: reparent yourself. This means that you take a good look at how you were parented as well as how you internalized the parenting. You begin to heal yourself from old wounds. You then consciously decide what works and what does not work in the way that you treat yourself. You eliminate negative patterns of behavior so that these are not automatically passed on to your children.

Number Two: you realize that you and your significant other are caregivers to your children, and as such are the models or mirrors that are reflecting the values, beliefs, and ways of being that your children will inevitably adopt. Therefore, you will review the way that you resolve conflict, communicate, and relate to your spouse or other significant caregivers. You will consciously take on new behavior that replaces ways of being that are not the way that you want your children to be reflected.

Number Three: you will then learn the skill of being a *Listener Of The Heart*, which is more than the skill of attentive listening—it is a way of listening which allows you to be fully present and ready and willing to discover, uncover, and empower your child's innate potential. Your aim is to develop their already existing potential in a way that does not break their will, but instead allows them to take their place in society as creative, self-expressed and confident individuals.

I believe that reading this book can open an individual to consider new aspects of what it means to raise a child that is whole and complete, and, therefore, can begin the process of conscious parenting. I do think that there are many disciplines that an individual can use as tools to become more conscious. However, to become a conscious parent who really listens and empowers their children, I believe this book will be very insightful, as it provides the actions to fulfill the joy of parenting.

Readers will have a shift in the way that they view their parenting job. The skill of **Listening With The Heart** creates a foundation of respect in the relationship between parent and child. You actually learn to listen, feel, and take actions that are merged with reason and love.

Parents will transform their relationship to themselves and have more ease, joy, and satisfaction personally as well in their roles as parents. The ability with which they learn to be present and to really listen to their children will assure a bond of love between parent and child throughout all stages of their development. The other results will be the ability to set healthy boundaries, communicate effectively with your child, and diminish tension, arguments, and disruption. Your child will have a secure and confident voice, which will translate into higher self-esteem, self-confidence, and self-worth.

PART I:

UNCONSCIOUS
PARENTING

Sleepwalking - Raising My Daughter

L et me tell you a story about being an unconscious parent. This story is not meant to be a judgment of being unaware, disinterested, or semi-present to the huge responsibility of raising a child. It is certainly not meant to judge anyone out there who has been unconscious or has been raised by unconscious parents themselves. The story is about me. My unconsciousness, my inability to be present to the huge challenge of motherhood is what I am referring to and not my deep love for my daughter, nor the amazing woman she is.

When I became pregnant at 18 years old, I did not have a committed desire to become a mother and to behold the sacred life of my little girl. It was the consequence of having had sex with my boyfriend, who was my first love. My daughter was born a healthy baby girl of 7 pounds and 11 ounces.

I got married in North Carolina to my daughter's dad under parental duress by the justice of the peace. I was three months pregnant. Nothing about that ceremony, nor the later church ceremony, was memorable. I was told that this was the right thing to do. He was my first love and I did love him. I was neither in acceptance nor in love with being a wife or a mother. I tried to imitate what other parents were doing. I read Dr. Spock's book on how to deal with a child at different stages of development and I fed my daughter and changed her. I took her to the babysitter's house religiously every morning before I went to work. She was a beautiful child who was gifted to me and who I was not prepared to receive.

I loved my husband, but marriage and playing house were not what I wanted to do. I wanted to continue with my education, and have fun. It was all one big "I." The outcome was that I separated from him when he was called into the armed services. This was during the last stages of the Vietnam War. He was discharged shortly after he was recruited because his father died. Seven months later, he was in a fatal car crash. He passed away at the age of 23. Now I was truly totally and utterly alone with my daughter, who was just 2 years old. I was on a roller coaster ride. The ride was mine. I took her along. When my daughter was 5, I decided to take her to Buenos Aires, Argentina. It seemed like a good idea. I was adventurous and in love again. At 24, I jumped at the idea of following a new love and sold everything I had in New York. I ran to catch the plane with her in hand, never thinking about the consequences this action could cause to my life or to hers. We flew across the world. This all illustrates the fact that an unconscious parent does not consider the needs of her children. I disregarded her need for safety and consistency and relationships with her loved ones, like her grandmother, who not only had lost her husband but lost her son.

In Argentina, we went to live in the city of La Plata where the man I had fallen in love with was living. I had met him on my first trip back to Argentina as an adult. He was a musician with a great deal of charm and I was a free-spirited young Argentine-born woman from the United States. There was an instant attraction. The passion was overwhelming and within a few months, I decided that I needed to be with him. He had just separated from his wife and had a little one-year-old boy. I quickly rented an incredible apartment in La Plata and made arrangements for my daughter to go to school. I didn't spend time with her; I was busy sorting out my love life. I remember being so unconscious that one time I forgot to pick her up at school and a neighbor brought her home. She never complained. She was a very sweet and bright little girl. She adapted quickly to school even when she had to learn Spanish. She excelled in sports.

I can imagine what she must have gone through, not only being in a foreign country but having her primary security, me, be so unpredictable and unstable. I remember vividly one night when we were living in Buenos Aires, I put her to bed around 9 p.m. and went across the street to a café to meet my boyfriend. I was gone for about 45 minutes. When I returned, my daughter was in a panic. She had woken up and hadn't found me. Shortly after this incident, she developed a phobia. She would panic if she was left alone in a room. Someone would always have to be with her. I took her to a psychologist for therapy. While through time she recovered from the effects of her fear, for years afterward, she was always concerned about my safety, and she continues to feel concerned about my well-being and safety to this day. While she knew I somehow would always be there for her, she became very alert to any kind of threat and worried a great deal.

My unconscious ways of parenting could have been devastating. I remember that my daughter and her little friend played together in front of our apartment house when we lived on Migueletes Street in Buenos Aires. That day she was wearing a cute light tan suede skirt and a yellow sweater. I remember it well because I was called downstairs by her friend who was screaming that someone had taken my daughter. I shot out of the house like a bullet and ran to find her. I found her in a small abandoned lot half a block away. A man was running from her. I picked her up and held her close. She told me that the man had asked her if she wanted candy and took her there. He hadn't harmed her physically but she was really scared. The thought of anyone or anything harming my daughter was not something I could live with. However, it was only at this extreme moment that I fully became conscious of my love and commitment to her. For a short time, I was totally present with her. I picked her up from school and did her homework with her. I tried to be the proper mother according to what I thought I should be. However, before long I was having some drama with a boyfriend and was absorbed by my feelings of hurt. Sometimes she would come over to me and try to comfort me. That was my job as a mother and I was not able to give her the safety and stability that she needed.

After 9 years living in Argentina, we returned to the United States in 1981. I was singing professionally at the time and I was advised by my own therapist to put my daughter in a boarding school. He said that this would be the safest route for her, and so she went off to boarding school in Massachusetts for two years. While I visited her at least once a month and she came home for holidays, I cannot remember any meetings with the nuns or phone calls or special outings with her.

I was still singing professionally and I had begun a psychotherapy practice when I took her out of boarding school and brought her back to New York to live with me.

While in New York, I placed her in a very prestigious school, but when she was not doing well in school, I did not spend time with her or help her work on her projects. I did not ask her what she needed. Her emotional needs were not a top concern for me. Now, it is clear that in no way was I callous or uncaring. I was just too self-absorbed to actually pay attention and to think about what she may have been going through. I was disappointed in her performance. After all, I sent her to another wonderful school in New York City, and in my mind, she was "screwing up." I wanted her to be a good girl and not give me any problems. She did this pretty well. However, the impact was that she did not have my guidance or support. She did not feel the safety of her mother's love and devotion to nurture her so that she could feel free to discover her natural gifts and talents.

When we lived in New York and she was going to high school, she found solace in a group of friends who worked on the horse and buggy rides in Central Park. Thank God she was always level-headed because at the age of 16 or 17 she had very little supervision. I cannot imagine today being this unconscious about raising a child or a young woman. My background, with its own lack of stability, left me unable to be aware of my daughter's need for security. As I look back at those parenting years now, I feel a mixture of disbelief and grief at what I missed with my precious daughter. I received an amazing gift in her birth but I was not aware nor able to receive it.

I wanted her to go to college; it was important to me that she get an education. At college, she met her first love and ignored her studies. I flew to her college town and spent two days completing her assignments so that she could do well. She didn't even bother to hand them in. It was I who wanted her to do well—I did not want to be a failure as a mother because my daughter did not succeed at college. Her performance in many ways, as I now look back, was also about me.

In the end, my daughter quit school and moved out on her own. She did things her way and she developed herself into an amazing woman.

I loved my daughter and I did, like my parents, the best I "knew how." This is not a justification. I know that I was not a "safe space" for her and undoubtedly it had its impact. Yet what I also discovered, as you read on, is that my daughter was born with a strength of spirit and unlimited potential that has been a huge resource in her life.

Love And Parenting Are Carried Down

The way we love ourselves and our children is carried down from one generation to the next.
The way we love is manifested in the way that we care, nurture and raise our children.

How do we automatically parent our children? We merely followed our society's guidelines at the time and modeled the way we were parented. In many cases, we just imitated others. We looked outside of ourselves for the guidelines to parenting instead of attempting to distinguish for ourselves what works best for each child. When parenting skills are passed down it is not experts we are listening to, but it is our inherited inner conversations that we have not examined. These societal standards are heard by us with a sense of "rightness." It is inevitable that we will keep passing down what we learned to our children unless we interrupt these automatic conversations. If we are not able to parent in a way that allows a child to preserve their wholeness, we will inevitably carry down the wholeness, we will inevitably carry down the inconsistencies, lack of self-worth, self-esteem, and confidence that we may have inherited. Becoming conscious parents is the pathway to abolish this lack of wholeness in future generations.

In sharing my mother's story, I would like to give you the opportunity to see how I unconsciously adopted and repeated with my own daughter the way I was parented.

My Mother's Story

At the age of 21, my mother made her debut as a leading soprano in the Opera House, El Teatro Colon, in Buenos Aires, Argentina. She was born into an Italian immigrant family. Her parents had four children.

Her father was a neighborhood barber. He loved the Opera and used to sit my mother on his lap and sing to her. She quickly began to sing back to him. She loved to play an imaginary piano. Even as a child, she had a beautiful voice.

When she was in her early teens, she became the protégé of a prominent singing teacher who took her under her wing. Singing was her primary focus when she became pregnant with me at the age of 26. She and my father were in love and were married secretly—my grandparents wanted her to only concentrate on her career. Since no one knew that she had married, when she became pregnant with me, I was also kept a secret since she feared that people would assume that I was illegitimate. She was swept away to the nearby city of Tandil, where I was born. It was not until I was one year old before anyone outside of the immediate family knew of my birth.

My mother and father never lived together. Shortly after I was born, they divorced. So, while I got a name and legitimacy, I did not get a family. My mother was busy with her career, so I rarely was with her. I remember her mostly on stage in the Opera. Even at such an early age, I remember having the feeling of not belonging.

Not belonging impacted me severely as a child and later as an unconscious parent. How? I never felt rooted. I never felt part of a family. A sense of self-worth and belonging were foreign to me. Although I wanted to belong, what was automatic was to keep moving from one thing to the next and, later, from one man to the next. This pattern was present when, like my mother, I became pregnant at an early age. My mother was not prepared to be a parent. And she and I never bonded.

History Repeats Itself

My mother had been offered a long contract as leading soprano with the Metropolitan Opera. It was when I was 6 years old that I left my native land, Argentina, with my mother and grandparents for New York City. I still remember the apartment on Central Park West. Initially, I was raised by my grandmother and grandfather; I was safe and relatively happy. I loved them. No matter where I was, if they were there, I felt safe and at home.

After a year passed, my mother met an American man and married him. He suggested that my grandparents return to Argentina and that my mother put me in a Catholic boarding school in New Jersey.

I remember the days before my grandparents left. The house was filled with suitcases and trunks. My grandmother was sewing labels on my clothes, blankets, and sheets. Nobody was telling me what was happening. I was anxious and scared. I walked around the large trunks that were being filled with clothes. When my grandparents left, I don't remember saying goodbye to them. My joy and aliveness seemed to be gone. I remember thinking "I must have been bad—that's why they are gone."

My mother put me in St. Mary's Academy. My third-grade teacher was a big scary nun who always seemed angry. I was a very inquisitive and free-spirited child when I arrived at St. Mary's Academy. I sang and played and ran around and knew very little about observing rules. I had been given a lot of love and freedom by my grandparents. I was not used to the rigid discipline of my new school. I was one of 9 boarders at the school. The others were day students. I was in trouble most of the time. I talked at night when the lights were out or ran down the halls. I would forget to put my clothes in the laundry or would sometimes talk back to the nuns. We were punished with the dreaded "hair brush." The nuns spanked us with the hairbrush when we disobeyed.

When I was 8, my grandmother died during the political unrest in Argentina. I cried and cried when my mother told me that my Abuela had died. I never got to see my grandfather again either; he died the year before I returned to Argentina as an adult with my daughter in 1971.

Reflections

As I reflect on my childhood today, I realize how we are all impacted by the decisions that our parents, grandparents, teachers, family members, and society impose on children. Personally, I can see how I was impacted by the loss of my loving grandparents, whom I related to as my real parents and the one area of unconditional safety in my life. When my grandparents left, I felt a deep sadness and fear. I remember saying to myself, "I was not a good girl." From that moment, I stopped being a vibrant, inquisitive, and creative child

---

and became a fearful, apprehensive and anxious one. My grandparents' unconditional love and support were gone.

The impact of this loss penetrated every area of my life. I hid my internal sadness. It was many years later that I discovered the pain that I kept reliving in my relationships. "Don't leave me alone, I'll be a good girl." "Don't you love me?" "What did I do?"

I longed for my grandparents and found it difficult to bond with my mother who was rehearsing, singing, and traveling while I was at St. Mary's Academy from 7-13 years of age. She took me out because she was having a baby. I was then put in a public school in New York City where I really felt I didn't belong. I wore the wrong clothes, I was not cool, and, to compensate for not belonging, I became studious. My mother was not singing after my brother was born, but she was unavailable. She was seriously depressed. I became "mother's helper." I thought that by helping her somehow I would get closer to her. There were moments when she would confide in me and share that she didn't know what to do. I felt close when she needed to talk and I would try to give her solutions. Shortly after her mood would change and she would become distant. I understand now that her moods were an expression of her deep discontent with her life. I was trying to be good and when I came home from school, I would take my brother out to the park or do the laundry. I thought somehow that if I helped she would be happy, and especially so with me. No doubt, we had good moments at home too.

My stepfather was adventurous and he would call us and say, "Get the car ready," and my brother and I would go to drive-in movies with them till 1 or 2 in the morning. It was fun. Although sometimes it would be hard to get up to go to school the next morning.

What I remember most when I look back is that there was no order in the house. There was no conversation regarding how I was doing or what happened at school. I did my own planning and it's a miracle that I did well in High School. I don't remember my parents being at graduation.

History Repeats - Third Generation

I can clearly see the parallels between how my mother parented me and how I parented my daughter.

My lack of stability influenced how I was unable to be aware of my daughter's need for security. The lack of stability in my childhood after my grandparents left the United States was mirrored in the instability I created in my own life when raising my daughter.

Like my mother, I was totally involved in my own career and ignored my child.

Like my mother, I put my daughter in boarding schools so that someone else had to take care of her—not me.

Like my mother, I was more concerned that my daughter be obedient than be free and alive and growing into her own self-expression.

My mother was more concerned that I didn't embarrass her in front of her friends, just as I was embarrassed when my daughter dropped out of college—I didn't look good. My lack of grounding and mentoring from a healthy mother and/or father made me look for love early in my life in a lover instead of finding it within myself.

Like my mother, I became pregnant when I was not emotionally able to be responsible for a child.

My mother didn't model nurturing or emotional connection for me and I didn't model it for my daughter.

As I look back at my years of parenting my daughter, I feel a mixture of disbelief and deep grief.

I am very blessed to this day to have such a wise, intelligent, and loving daughter. She has created a warm and healthy life. We have discussed our past several times and, when I ask her what it was like to have me as a mother, she does not share any negative feelings. She says, "You did the best you could!" Yes, we all do. I say sometimes in certain areas of developing our children, we can recognize that doing the best one can is not a justification for it not being in the best interest of our children's optimal development.

Cleaning Up With My Daughter

I was in psychotherapy a few years before my son was born when I awakened to what it must have been like for my daughter to have me as a mother. I felt a tremendous loss. How could I have been so unconscious? It was at this time that I was able to make amends with my daughter who by then was 16 years old. I got in touch with the fact that 16 years had gone by and I had not really been there emotionally for her. I apologized to her.

I remember that day as if it were a minute ago. I sat with her on my bed and asked her to forgive me.

"I am really sorry that I wasn't there for you."

"Mom," she took my hand, *"we have the rest of our lives."*

I appreciated what she said, but I knew she had been heartbreakingly lonely many, many times growing up "without" me.

One night, I called to ask my daughter, "What was it like to have me as a mother?" At first, she laughed and then she said that she didn't think that she really had it so bad. She enjoyed most of the time we'd spent in Argentina. We remembered our lives there like the time we brought home several little yellow chicks and a few days later I got home to find her eating baked chicken I'd made while playing with the baby chicks. Or the time we walked 35 kilometers to see Juan Peron when he returned to Argentina. Thousands of people packed the roads to meet him at the airport. Snipers started shooting and the crowd panicked. We grabbed a small tree and hung on. Without the tree, we would have been trampled over. When I shared this with her, she became silent.

"Are you okay?"

I told her about a letter that she had sent me when she was 10 and living with her paternal grandmother in New

York for two months. I'd forgotten about it for 30 years and only just recently found it in an old trunk. I remember the pain I felt when I read the words again with a new ability to feel the loneliness behind the written words:

> *"Mom, I am okay. I think about you and miss you. I wonder, do you miss me too?*

She was crying. Back in her mind; she was the little girl who worried that she was a burden to me. I cried too, because, if I was really honest about having a child then, she had been a burden instead of a gift to me.

She told me that she has always felt that, if things go really well for her, they wouldn't stay that way. "I feel that I don't deserve to be really happy." At that moment I fully understood how we inherit our patterns of behavior. I had passed on to her the same patterns that had been passed on to me. I interpreted the loss of my grandparents and the absence of a mother and father as "unworthy to be loved." She inherited this story unexamined when she was young and lived in her own world of "not being loved" or "being wanted." Of course, this was not the truth, and yet human beings seem to translate at a young age that love is shown when your dear ones want to spend time with you when they are present and show their nurturing and care.

The good news is that I have been able to reverse or clear out these patterns with myself and with her. In spite of our difficult journey together, we have a very close relationship. She lives a healthy life and is clear about how to deal with who she is in the world. She has a wonderful loving husband. She is very intelligent and has created a life that she loves.

Discovering the Unconscious Parent

W *hat is the Unconscious Parent?*

Unconscious Parents are not always aware and nurturing of the emotional needs of their children. They are not fully aware that they are the primary nurturers of their children's physical, mental, emotional, and spiritual capacities.

The Unconscious Parent is someone who has not yet been awakened to the fact that they are raising their children the same way that they were raised. If negative patterns of behavior were modeled in the past, these are merely carried down to the next generation. History repeats itself only when we have not taken the time to reflect on and break up old inherited behaviors.

Unconscious Parents are fervently focused on adapting their children to the world and the particular society and norms that they are living in. Parenting practices are set to give them the skills and standards in their existing world so that they can survive in the world as the parents know it to be. How they feel, how they think, and what matters to them may not be viewed as essential to children's growth and maturity. As a matter of fact, their personal objections or needs are viewed as a disturbance to many parents who are not aware and who understandably are doing everything to give them the best they know. These parents may be well-educated, responsible, loving individuals who are still sleepwalking. They are inside the current world and follow the rules. They very rarely question themselves about the way they are parenting. They look for new techniques and tools to fix their children when they are not performing; however, very rarely do they question that the society and the standards they and teachers are imposing may not be appropriate for their child.

Unconscious Parents may only take care of children's basic needs to survive in the world. It is clear that in my "sleepwalking phase" bringing up my daughter, I was only focused on taking care of her physical needs. I knew that she needed to go to school and have friends and go to bed at a certain time and eat her meals. I felt good because she went to good schools and she enrolled in gymnastics and swimming and dance. I was a dutiful mother, but, as I mentioned before, I was only being responsible for a small portion of my daughter's development because I was ignoring all the qualities and wisdom that she was bringing with her to the world. I was not discovering her.

Unconscious Parents may fail to develop a strong bond with the child. There is nothing wrong with this type of parenting. I remember giving a lecture in a school some time ago, and a father stood up and said: "I'll tell you what works. When my son misbehaves, I just give him one of these." He showed me his fist. "It worked on me, and it sure shuts him up." I explained to him that the way he and I were brought up was effective because intimidation, fear, and even physical punishment would ensure obedience. It just fails to create an emotional connection between parent and child. It is focused on trying to get the "little creatures" to obey. When children obey out of fear, they are avoiding the wrath of the parent rather than buying into the value of what the parent may want to contribute. If there is no discussion or exchange of ideas, the child will succumb to the will of the parent but not embrace the lesson the parent wants to give. Even worse, they may grow resentful of the parent.

Unconscious Parents raise children to be obedient. "Good little children do as they are told and never object." They may be well-mannered, kind, and considerate. In fact, they are sleepwalking little robots that are there to please Mom and Dad and fit into the world according to the social and class structure of their parents. They are there to fulfill the dreams and ideas of their parents. They are treated as objects. They go where they are told. They do as they are told. They don't have a voice. By this, I mean that they are not asked to express their thoughts, feelings, and ideas, which are so vital to developing autonomy, self-confidence, and self-trust.

Unconscious Parents may shame, hit, shout, and scream at their children. It is understandable that many times parents are frustrated because they must work hard to manage the home and they want peace and quiet. However, screaming, hitting, etc. does not help the child to understand. This is misleading communication. It is damaging and hurtful which is not what the parent wants.

Basically, in **Unconscious Parenting,** there is very little communication. This leads to eventual rebellion and resentment, especially during adolescence.

If they dare to say something that is contrary or confronts what is being offered by the parents, they may be labeled as "difficult children." The more difficult they are, the more they are punished and ridiculed. The focus is not on what could be happening to my child that they aren't communicating, but rather how can this difficult child be fixed so that I don't have to deal with this issue. The parents then may turn to professionals to fix the problems, often not realizing that there is little "listening" going on in the home. Or in most cases whatever the issues are, they never get resolved.

The Unconscious Parent is not aware of the importance of spending time with the child to find out for themselves what the problem is. While all of this is understandable since we are only human, it has an impact. The impact of not dealing with your child's thoughts and feelings can leave them with an internal dialogue: "I don't matter" or "I am a bother" or many other things that we repress and don't express.

Unconscious Parents have expectations of their children without training them to develop their self-reliance, responsibility, or self-confidence. It seems that all of the sudden at a certain age, perhaps around 17 or 18, a child is supposed to be responsible for their money, job, career, studies, etc. when they have spent their lives depending on a parent or being on their own without any guidance. How can they develop these attitudes when they are not nurtured from a very young age? When the child is not mentored from young, it is unfair to expect them to have acquired these traits. The child may have a great deal of book education but is lacking in discovering their worth from engaging in productive conversations with parents.

Unconscious Parents may not discover their child's inherent gifts and talents, which can be the key elements for them to find their vocation and fulfillment in life. Without discovering our own voice, we are limited in the depth of our contribution to ourselves and to others. Children may have kept within the dictated guidelines, but internally anger and resentment create distance between parent and child. This parenting style can create dissatisfied, unhappy individuals who, at their core, may be playing the game of life and are viewed as "winners" but are in fact living a double life: an outer life lived according to the rules so that they fit in and look good, and an inner life of suppressed feelings, wants, and needs.

Unconscious Parents say, "I love my kids; there is nothing I wouldn't do for them." I believe **Unconscious Parents** say this with all their hearts. Many of us who were raised by **Unconscious Parents**—myself included—have not authentically developed self-confidence and trust. We may show a personality that is confident or self-assured, while inside there is always a doubting voice that we may live with. "Am I good enough?" "Will I be liked?" "What's wrong with me?" "Will I ever be truly loved?"

The Unconscious Parent does not engage in conversations for discovering their child. We give advice to our children and are well-meaning. However, we don't really know who our children are because we do not really engage our children in deep conversations to discover what they think or feel. As **Unconscious Parents,** we do not know that our children can offer us insights into living. Children are viewed as incomplete until they reach adulthood and the measurement is chronological age.

The Unconscious Parent may only express approval or their love when the child is meeting the rules and plans of the parent. If the child fulfills the expectations of the standards and ideals of the parents, then they get the reward of the parents' love and approval. If, however, they get into problems and are acting out in any way, the love is withdrawn. The behavior is not dealt with as undesirable, but the child is dealt with as bad and wrong and the withdrawal of love is the consequence. The child lives in a seesaw of trying to find who he or she is while at the same time avoiding the punishment of the parent. This results in not being able to communicate or learn what could be a valuable lesson for living.

The Unconscious Parent may threaten or bribe their children to get them to obey. The parents who may want to get their children to behave may threaten them. I know of a case where the father stopped the car and pulled his son out and left him in the middle of the road. Of course, he came back and the boy was quiet. However, nothing was resolved. Intimidation and fear was the only thing present. This manipulation can get the desired results but alienates the parent and child more and more until there is no connection left. It also does not work to bribe the child. "If you stop asking me and if you are good, then I will buy you a toy." This does not teach the child anything other than to learn to manipulate the parent so that they can get what they want. This can lead to delinquent behavior and false entitlement in the later years.

The Unconscious Parent can transition into a Conscious Parent. While it may sound like I am very critical of **Unconscious Parents**, I am not. My intention is for all of us parents to awaken to a more effective way of parenting our children. If you are reading this book, you may see yourself in what I am sharing. The good news is that we can step into becoming **Conscious Parents**. This new way of being will not only make the parenting job easier and more joyful, but our children will be raised with a higher level of confidence and self-esteem. This undoubtedly will, in turn, not only contribute to them but to the society that we live in. The key is the following: Unless we are willing to reflect and question our behaviors and actions as parents, we cannot step into **Conscious Parenting**.

Reflections

Parenting for obedience stifles creativity. It does not open the vast possibility of allowing the child to explore the many views of life. The child is limited to thinking only about how they can get the "right" answer to achieve goals that are already given by society. Their ability to think for themselves is diminished or halted.

Not having conversations with your children and asking them "what do you see" and "what do you think" at any stage of development does not give room for them to share their feelings and inner world. This can lead to a lack of depth, sadness, lack of self-worth, insecurity, self-confidence, and deadness of spirit.

PART II:

CONSCIOUS PARENTING

Awakening: How I Became a Conscious Parent

Healing from my past began when I was desperately lost and arrived with my daughter in Argentina. I was alone with her and had looked for love in the arms of unavailable men. I started going to psychotherapy. In these sessions, while I was still studying Psychology, I became very aware of my emotional wounds as a child and my desperate need to be loved and to belong. I realized that leaving Argentina at such a young age and losing my grandparents, who, for me, were all the safety and security I had known, left a huge void in me which resulted in feelings of abandonment and loss. Through my studies and weekly sessions over the period of many years, I was able to begin to affirm my self-confidence and self-esteem. I was also able to begin to see how I had been repeating my mother's story and how not having an available dad led me to not trust a man as someone who could protect me. I was also able to forgive myself for being a young mother who was scared and ill-equipped to be a stable parent. When I moved back to the

United States, I continued to read many books and completed workshops on how children develop and this continued to help me understand how we develop from childhood and the impact our caretakers and education, or lack of it, have on who we become. I also became more aware of how certain character traits get carried down from generation to generation when our life stories are not explored and healed.

In 1985, I was introduced to various alternative therapies such as energy healing. I awakened to a new realm of understanding. I trusted myself to listen to my intuition. What I call intuition is a quiet inner counsel which is a deep attentive listening. This newfound confidence in myself grew. Every morning I would open a blank page in my diary and allow a free stream of consciousness to fill the page. Through this practice, I developed a trust in listening to the wisdom within me.

I took part in a training program that became a cornerstone to my becoming a true "creator" of my life. This ontological exploration with 200 other people provided me with a first-hand view of how as human beings, regardless of where we are born, our ethnic, or our cultural background, become programmed into a world of survival. In this powerful course, I realized that I had the power to create my life and that I was not limited to the way I became as a personality through my life experiences.

I had deep concerns for the human spirit and the soul of each of us. I explored many spiritual practices such as meditation to quiet the mind, deep listening practices, yoga, spending time in nature, storytelling, and voice work in groups called toning. I also became interested in exploring practical Christianity. I began to be more and more in tune with my connection to everything and everyone. In these studies, I developed a deeper compassion for myself and other human beings. I began to be able to resonate with what others were feeling or experiencing in a deeper way than ever before. I noticed that my relationships now included an intimacy level of the heart that transcended the obvious or the material dimension.

As my son grew, I would include rituals of meditating as a family; always asking him what he thought and making sure that he trusted himself. From a very young age, when he had to make a decision, I would tell him to close his eyes and listen for the answer. This became a practice for him throughout his young years.

Unfortunately, my son's father and I wanted different things which led us to separate and divorce. However, what gave us the power and ability to keep focused on our son's well-being was some of the deep respect that we had for each other as well as our love for him. Many years after our divorce I realized that it is extremely important to have effective communication skills and conflict resolution skills in a marriage. This led me to explore these skills as well.

Alternative Therapies for Awakening

*Stream of Consciousness Journaling- The term "stream of consciousness" originated in William James' "The Principles of Psychology." Stream of consciousness writing is a technique in which the writer continually writes their thoughts out without pause. Once written out, one can track the writers' fluid mental state. This is especially useful during the process of awakening. It provides a map of one's consciousness in a particular moment. If you feel called to work through something that has felt particularly jumbled in your mind this practice can help you to sort through your thoughts in a non-judgemental and all-encompassing way.

*Meditation to Quiet the Mind- Merriam-Webster provides one definition for meditation: "to engage in mental exercise (such as concentration on one's breathing or repetition of a mantra) for the purpose of reaching a heightened level of spiritual awareness." There are many styles of meditation. Focusing on the breathing, a mantra, or utilizing a guided meditation can be especially useful in quieting the mind. You do not have to be void of thoughts to engage in mediation. Instead, let passing thoughts flow and refocus on your breath, manta, or guide. This is the first step in gaining the ability to quiet your mind at will.

*Deep Listening Practice- Deep listening is the act of suspending judgment and being fully present with the speaker. This involves more than hearing but actively searching for the underlying meaning. By doing so, one can better empathize with the speaker by picking up on unspoken needs or feelings. You can also practice deep listening with yourself by analyzing your own thoughts or reactions. Being gentle with yourself and others and taking the extra step to listen to the unspoken will transform how you communicate.

*Yoga- Yoga is Hindu spiritual and ascetic discipline made up of asanas (postures), meditation and breathwork. Often referred to as a moving meditation, yoga is another practice to aid in quieting the mind and tuning into one's consciousness.

*Communion with Nature- Stillness in the natural world contributes to both emotional and physical well-being. Studies show that time in nature reduces blood pressure, heart rate, muscle tension, and the production of stress hormones.

*Storytelling- Getting in touch with your own story is a vital part of awakening. Telling your story in a meaningful way can be healing. Displaying your truth to others unabashedly builds confidence in one's authentic self. Meaningful storytelling doesn't have to include a large audience. Simply sharing your story with a trusted loved one can be transformational.

*Toning- Toning is a practice of creating sound by using the voice to make tones and frequencies. Our voices are essential to self-expression. Getting in tune with your true voice increases your ability to express yourself. Sound can help manage our emotional state, releasing stuck energy in the body through the voice. Toning is also a form of mediation and can be especially useful for those that find silent meditation difficult to focus on.

Raising My Son

Speaking about being a **Conscious Parent** does not mean that I was always super present or that I "wore a halo and wings." It means that I had explored much of my past parenting and released my past hurts that I held against myself and my mother and father. I had looked at myself long and hard and I had blossomed into a more compassionate, nurturing woman. I was ready at the onset of pregnancy to welcome wholeheartedly all of the challenges and the joys of giving life to another human being.

When I met my son's father, I was on contract to sing at a prestigious hotel in Bermuda. He was the Assistant Manager there and literally checked me in when I arrived for my 5-week performing engagement. He was attractive, energetic, and had a great lighthearted sense of fun. It took a very short time for us to bond. When I finished my singing contract, I went back to New York, and, after many phone calls, I decided that I wanted to pursue the relationship. So, I went to Bermuda to live with him. We married in Bermuda on February 14, 1983. It was a small but beautiful wedding. When he got his resident visa for the U.S., we moved to New York City.

By 1985, we were ready to have a child. We had named our son almost three years before he was born. He was a healthy baby of 8 pounds 3 ounces who was bald for a long time and reminded me of a little Buddha. Giving birth to my son was so different from when I had my daughter. I had my hand held tightly by my husband throughout the natural childbirth. I remember being fully awake and concerned that my son had all of his fingers and toes. When he arrived with arms flinging, his dad held him for the first time while I anxiously awaited to see that all was well. He indeed was very healthy and well.

My experience of being with my son was sacred to me. I made sure that I was with him even when I went back to work. I worked Tuesdays, Wednesdays, and Thursdays and kept Mondays and Fridays free to be home with him. Definitely a strong difference from when I had my daughter and all I could think of was being out of the house. I enjoyed every moment with him. I gave him baths and made sure he had about ten toys in the bathtub. His

Dad read to him every night. We definitely loved him. Even while we were struggling financially, nothing contaminated the way we loved him. We have always said that our son is the best of both of us. But as we poured our love into him, we forgot to care for each other. By the time our son was 5, his father and I were growing apart. We did not communicate and there was a growing sense of resentment between us. This resulted in our separation and later divorce.

During our separation, my son faced a difficult situation. Not only did he have to deal with the fact that his dad was no longer living with us, but shortly after our separation, I was offered an opportunity to work again on the beautiful island of Bermuda. This time, the job was not as a professional singer but as a clinical psychologist. After a great deal of reflection and discussion with his father and a child psychologist, his father consented with us moving to Bermuda. We made arrangements for our son to speak to him every day.

During the course of the following two years, especially at bedtime, my son would get what we labeled as "the daddy feeling," a deep sense of loss and anxiety from missing his dad. While he adjusted to his new life, I sat with him and listened and comforted and reassured him. The key was how present and how empathetic I was. I resonated with his feelings while still staying clear and strong in the knowledge that he would make it through his mourning period.

His dad remarried about the same time that our son was no longer mourning the loss of having his dad near him. From my perspective, my son was relieved to know that his father was no longer alone. I think his inner struggle dissolved naturally, through our nightly conversations and heartfelt exchanges. I reassured him that "Dad loves you very much and will always be there for you, no matter what happens." I assert that it was because he maintained a strong relationship with his dad, even while he lived away, and because he was able to openly share his thoughts and feelings, his self-esteem and his ability to grow into a strong and well-adjusted young man were not hindered.

I loved being his mother. There was nothing that was more important to me. I enjoyed discovering who he was and every morning was a new adventure for me. He was the most important thing in my life. When I was raising my daughter, "I" was the most important thing in my life. My insecurities, my adventures, and finding a new love were more important than what was happening in her life. As a result of being a **Conscious Parent**, my experience of my son and our relationship created an openness that, in my view, gave him the space to excel and succeed. For example, I do not recall him having to tell him to go to bed or do his homework. He loved to go to school and was very conscientious about playing by the rules, doing his homework, and going to bed when it was time. When he was 9, he took the bus home from school by himself and, when I came home a half-hour later, he'd still have his school blazer on while sitting at the dining room table doing his homework. I'd ask him if he'd had a snack and he'd reply, "No, mom, I have to do my homework." Parenting him was easier because I approached my relationship with respect even when he was a young boy.

I believe that my **Conscious Parenting** was what motivated him to flourish. I still went out with friends and had a personal life, but the way I was connected to him gave him safety and security. I listened to him and let him know that he was loved. There was no need to have strict rules. He did not have to fight for attention. He had it when he needed it.

At the same time, I was aware that I needed to establish healthy boundaries. For example, when he was around 13 years old, we had an argument and he was rude to me. I needed to establish a boundary that such behavior is not okay. So, I told him to take a walk around the block and locked him out of the house. Being a defiant teenager, he then tried to go around to the other side of the house and find an alternative entrance back into the house, but as he opened the terrace door, I found him. As we stared at each other, we both burst into laughter and then we sat down and had a conversation where he apologized for speaking rudely to me. Through the years, I have tried to foster a relationship where we would sit down and talk whenever we had a disagreement.

Doing homework was fun. We sat together and I enjoyed looking over his work. This continued into high school when he went to Prep Boarding School. I would find out what he needed to read and read the same books and discussed them with him. No matter how old, I always found a way to connect with him. Even when he traveled as a boy, I remember making two animals by hand that he took with him on trips from the ages of 6-8 years old. One was named "Weirdo" because he really looked weird. We still laugh about this.

Outcomes of Conscious Parenting:

1. Closely observing a child and asking questions allows for a strong sense of self and personal worth.

2. Interacting with my son was fundamental for him to voice himself. While I may not always agree or give him his way, he was never invalidated nor censored in expressing himself.

3. My constant discovery of his potential and desires prompted me to open doors for him. These may have been in sports, education, or in his emotional and personal interactions.

4. Having constant conversations with him gave a mutual connection and level of intimacy that allowed him to think deeply for himself. He was able to have time to think through what he was dealing with.

5. The practice of having him look within himself for the answers to any issue he may face gave him a strong reference point to always rely on.

Reflections on My Son's Parenting Experience

My son has provided his own thoughts on how I parented him: "When I look back at how my mother parented me, the one thing that stands out is that she helped instill me with inner confidence. No matter the task or challenge, I felt like my mom was there to support me to overcome it, but also I felt like I could do it too. In the end, my mom helped open doors for me as a parent, but also guided me and gave me the space to walk through them on my own.

Raising My Son's Spiritual/Intuitive Intelligence

As I kept studying and practicing many religious and spiritual disciplines, I realized that all children are born with an innate wisdom that needs to be nurtured from a young age. From the time my son was able to talk, I would ask him deep questions about life to prompt him to look within for the answer. For example, when he was four, I would ask, "What is the most important thing in life?" He would say "Love," "family" or perhaps even "God." When I asked him what God is he would say, "God makes the flowers grow." My own curiosity about how he would respond both allowed us to develop a more intimate relationship but also allowed him to realize that he had the answers.

Dee's Reflections

My heart overflowed with joy no matter what parenting challenges I faced raising my son. But how was I different than when I was raising my daughter?

Yes, I was older. However, being older does not necessarily make you more conscious. I was more conscious because I had shed my resentments of not having had the "perfect" childhood. I had made amends with my mother and father. I had stopped being a victim of my past and I now had the tools to live my life in the present moment more freely, rather than in my internal drama. I enjoyed being a mother and did not see it as a chore. I was not stifled by having to be there for my child. I saw being a mother as an adventure. The adventure was the discovery of the life I was the guardian of. I was open to love. This is what made me a more **Conscious Parent** with my son. It took having to deal with my divorce for me to fully realize the intricacies of love and commitment. I know now that **Conscious Parents** are obligated to know how to listen and to resolve conflicts with their spouses.

When you divorce and you have children, whatever conflicts were not resolved in the marriage are present in the divorce, and the child remains caught in the middle. It took me a few years to realize that, even divorced, our relationship was imperative to the wellbeing of our son.

Conscious Parents, even when divorced, learn how to parent effectively.

Characteristics of the Conscious Parent

A Conscious Parent is committed to parenting their children, knowing that they were born unique, whole, and complete. If they have characteristics that may be classified as "abnormal" or "out of the norm", they are not defective. A child is complete "as is" even when our definition of normality does not match their characteristics. At each stage of their development, we must be aware of what they are dealing with emotionally so that we can be present to any struggle that they may go through in life, especially when they are labeled by society as not "normal." Our philosophical foundation as parents is that they come to us at birth with the potential that we will assist them to develop.

A Conscious Parent knows that a child is worthy of respect from birth. Adulthood does not define when we are worthy of respect. A child is always worthy of being heard. Their thoughts, feelings, needs, and dreams are always worthy of being given the room to exist even if the parent ultimately cannot take care of what they want. At the very least, being heard and empathizing with the child expresses to them that their existence is valued.

The Conscious Parent knows that the child is distinctly independent of the parents' expectations. The parent discovers their child, the particular attitudes of the child from birth, and rather than fixing the child to fit society, the parent focuses on the development of those unique qualities and opens appropriate doors in society where the child can nurture such qualities.

A Conscious Parent assists the child in being a member of society without breaking his will. This guideline goes hand in hand with the one above. Whatever quality the child displays, for example: being energetic or loud, the parent makes sure that neither they nor or any of the caregivers make their ways of being wrong and try to explain that in certain environments a different type of behavior is required.

A Conscious Parent has taken the time to reflect and review their personal attitudes, values, beliefs, actions, and behaviors. They take the time to heal emotional wounds so as not to pass down outdated and ingrained past traumas to their children. We must display consistent boundaries for our children to feel safe and, at the same time, be flexible to discuss with them.

The gift that each child brings shows us the way to unconditional love.
It is up to us to choose to receive the gift.

The Conscious Parent never seeks to break the will of the child. They collaborate with the child to resolve problems and to find solutions by respecting and listening to the child's needs and wants, regardless of whether the needs can be met, not as impenetrable or rigid rules, but guidelines for parenting.

A Conscious Parent has developed their relationship with their spouse or significant other so as to learn healthy communication. Many problems arise in the home because parents consistently argue and do not resolve issues. This becomes an unsafe and toxic environment for the children to live in. Therefore, it is fundamental that the parents, whether together or apart, have communication skills that do not disrupt the well-being of the children.

A Conscious Parent has developed healthy boundaries. The cornerstone for raising children who develop high self-esteem and self-expression is mutual respect. Towards this goal, parents are truthful and open with their children. This openness is the foundation for building trust and safety. However, it is not a rigid authoritative figure who says, "Do as I say." Instead, the parent knows their boundaries so that they can engage with, but not fear being dominated by, the child. While the parent gives the child a voice, the parents make the final decisions until the child reaches adulthood.

PART III:

HOW TO BECOME A CONSCIOUS PARENT

Healing Ourselves: Discovering Our Inner Parent and Inner Child

I ask you to take time to look at yourself honestly and authentically so that you can slowly become conscious of what behaviors are valuable in you and which you would like to discard or change. These exercises are not meant to lay blame on anyone. However, if by taking this inventory you do have certain feelings of love, anger, disappointment, frustration, or sadness, let them be. They are or have been feelings that attached to your life experiences. Let your emotional body drain and eliminate these feelings organically.

The first step to changing our habits and behavior is to look at "what is so" in our lives. In order to become conscious, we have to awaken to the hidden and automatic ways of being and acting that are dictating our lives. Why do some people seek to discover new answers while others keep repeating the same errors throughout their lifetimes? This is indeed an abstract question. What we do know is that at certain points in our lives we are either nudged or shaken by events to break out of our automatic responses to living, or we are not. Sometimes it occurs because we meet with a tragic event. Other times someone or something touches us in a very special way. Perhaps for you, it will be reading this book.

I would like you to get present to the internal conversations that I will call your **Inner Parent** and your **Inner Child**.

The **Inner Parent** refers to the internalized voices and messages of the actual parent or caregivers. As we become adults, the inner conversations that guide us, give us counseling, confidence in our abilities or those internal conversations that make us feel guilty, ashamed or tells us whether to take a risk or not, is the voice of the **Inner Parent**.

Discovering these parental voices within us, will give us a choice as to whether we continue with taking action from these inner conversations or activate new voices.

I would like to offer that you also get present to the conversations of your **Inner Child**.

The **Inner Child** includes the characteristics of your true self as well as experiences as a child. These experiences are filled with wonder and joy as well as those that created wounds. These wounds have you react with hurt, anger and fear.

As you discover the characteristics of the **Inner Parent** and **Inner Child**, you will be able to access the pathways to **Conscious Parenting**. These are accessed by you being willing to look at your inner conversations that you are as a parent and the conversations that you internalized as a child.

You will begin to re-parent yourself and, in turn, parent your children with an open heart. Your heart will open when you have discovered and embraced the fear, hurt, anger and resentment that has clogged the flow of your love. You then create a new way to parent yourself through love. A *Listener Of The Heart* has accessed compassion for themselves, others and all life.

Connecting to love in action requires peeling away the negative views of yourself.

We start by remembering our childhood and making contact with the little inner boy or girl. This child still lives within you, no matter what age you are. Think back – maybe he or she disliked being wrong, being criticized, being disapproved of. This child may have worked hard or not at all to fit in. They probably gave up parts of themselves to fit in and have been successful or not, according to your society's rules. This child is short or tall. They are playful or sad. They come from any part of the world. They were loved or molested and neglected. What is true about this child is that they are either happy or not on a consistent basis because they feel valued and loved, or not. After all the trying to "be" someone who is worthy to fit in, to belong, to be loved and accepted, they will continuously be driven to find out who they are in the world by society's expectations and life's circumstances rather than to develop their worth from within.

Re-parenting Ourselves: Healing Our Past Wounds to Become Conscious Parents

You were programmed from birth to view your parent's behavior as a model or template to develop your own style of behavior. Watching them was your way of learning how to become an adult. With regard to the physical world, when you were born, your mind was like a blank computer disc. Your mother and your father simultaneously began to put new information into your data bank. For example, if your father was emotionally cool and your mother was emotionally warm, you will take on the combination of these two characteristics. It is also true that, if your grandparents, or uncles, or various caregivers were a strong influence in your early childhood, you will have taken on some of their characteristics. As you grow, you add on to this programming information from TV and other media. Your teachers and your ethnic and cultural surroundings also keep adding information to your computer bank. All of these experiences, whether conscious or unconscious, help to form your **Inner Parent**.

The Inner Parent and the Inner Child

When I make reference to the **Inner Child**, it's those behaviors you express that are full of wonder or full of pain. They live in the expression of your child-like self. All of us have an inner child. Some of us display an **Inner Child** when we are adults that are playful and fun, while the traumatized or emotionally injured inner child can display defensive, reactive and wounded behaviors.

Example: you may have had an experience as a child of being scolded in front of a classroom of children because you forgot your homework. The child feels ashamed and embarrassed. Then on top of what happened, the child may say to himself, "I'm not smart, I'm bad." And from that moment stops participating in life and lives from that decision. As an adult, the conversations of the **Inner Child** are still there and may be triggered when he experiences a situation of being reprimanded. Instead of responding to what is actually occurring now, the adult responds as a child and may quit his job or react with the anger repressed from the child.

However, as we look at these conversations of the **Inner Child** and allow this embarrassment and hurt from the past be expressed now, anyone can find more freedom to be present in life.

Your Inner Child's wounded self can be healed as you are willing to take an active role as your own caregiver and heal your past childhood wounds. You will find the empathy and connection you needed and didn't get from your parents or caregivers.

You must learn to comfort the inner pain that was not expressed or was not heard as you grew up.

When you get present to your own **Inner Child** and your childhood and bring love and compassion, you are not only acknowledging your **Inner Child**, but also opening yourself to see your own children as needing your empathy and compassion in dealing with their failures and challenges rather than your punishment.

69

As we heal ourselves, we become more empathetic to the difficulties and tears of our own children.

Exercise:

Find a picture of yourself as a child and put it on your nightstand. Every day say to that boy or girl: "I love you and am here for you no matter what!"

Listen to Your Inner Chatter

When we are adults, it is imperative to become aware of our parenting tapes, which we hear internally as thoughts, and develop new behaviors which will not only allow us to feel more self-acceptance but will also give way for our love to be expressed to everyone around us.

The first step is to begin taking inventory of what your inner conversations are like—you know, the chatter that goes on inside all day long and sometimes even when we are trying to sleep. These conversations can go on like this:

"You forgot to clean out the closet."

"Well, you never do what you say you are going to do."

"It doesn't matter, I can get to it another time."

"Yes, you've said that how many times and still never do it?"

"Well what's the big deal, it's only a closet."

"There you go again."

"Okay, I'll do it for sure by tomorrow. I have to get some sleep."

Some of you reading this book may be having an inner conversation that sounds like this:

"What is she talking about?"

"She must think I'm crazy."

"Let me see, am I talking to myself?"

"Yeah, I thought I was just thinking."

"Okay, so it's like talking under my breath."

"Now I get it, I didn't think of this before."

Most of us do not pay attention or are unaware of the fact that these inner conversations are taking place all the time. They occur when you are reading, eating dinner, watching television, sitting and looking out the window, making love, riding in the car, walking the dog, and most definitely when looking in the mirror or during any other activity that you can name.

These inner conversations can become not only repetitive, but they can also grow to be your emotional and mental staple diet. You can repeat the same inner conversations about yourself, about others, and your life for years. Unless you reflect on their validity and take responsibility for this internal dialogue, you will find you believe them and that they are driving your outlook and your choices.

Try to observe your inner conversations. It is easy to observe and even record outer conversations between individuals. However, because your inner conversations are inside your own mind, you must pay very close attention.

When you are particularly under stress you may be more aware of your inner conversations. Let's say you are waiting for your teenage son to come home as he promised at 12:00 a.m. and it is now 1:00 a.m.:

> *"Oh, God! Where's my baby?"*
>
> *"Don't worry, he's is fine."*
>
> *"But it's 1:00 a.m. and he's not home yet."*
>
> *"He's probably just having fun and forgot the time."*
>
> *"I'm going to give him a piece of my mind when he get's home."*
>
> *"Calm down, you don't want to start a fight."*
>
> *"What if he's hurt?"*
>
> *"If he's hurt, I could never get over it."*
>
> *"He's a good boy and trustworthy. Relax, he'll be home soon."*
>
> *"I'm going to call his friend and find out if he is with him."*

"At least wait another half hour before you do that."

"I'm going to call the hospital."

"Maybe you better calm down." (telephone rings)

"Oh God, maybe it's the hospital."

"Answer the phone, will you?"

Your inner conversations have participants with two distinct points of view, and they even speak in different tones. A common internal dialogue happens between your **Inner Parent** and your **Inner Child**. This **Inner Child** is distinguished into two parts: the conditioned **Inner Child** and the free wondrous child. I am referring here to the conditioned **Inner Child**.

As I mentioned before, when you were young, you internalized the personalities of your mother and your father or whoever the individuals were who were your primary caregivers. As part of your normal process of human development you internalized their behavior. Approximately by the age of seven, you absorbed your parent's ideas, mannerisms, viewpoints, energy levels, moods, nervousness, etc. These attitudes and beliefs became the composite of what we will call your **Inner Parent**.

As a child, you also developed your own point of view and outlook on life according to your experience at each stage of your development. You judged and formed a set of opinions and reactions to your parents and the world around you. Right or wrong, you made decisions about yourself and about your parents. Today, these voices act or react within you just the same way as when you were young. You may be chronologically 30, 40, 50, or even 80, but that voice still lives within you as your **Inner Child**.

Examining Our Internalized Parenting Model

Take a moment and read the following, or have someone read it to you.

Pay attention to your breath. Pay attention to your breath as it slowly enters and expands your belly and rib cage and then contracts as you exhale. Imagine that you are putting your external circumstances on hold, and you are just focusing within. Now take a trip down memory lane. Slowly go back in time to your high school days. Slow down and remember how you felt, and what you felt like at home. What was your relationship with your mom or dad like (whether they lived with you or not)? What did you want from them? What did you need? Did you get it, or did you act out and react to needing something that you could not get? Were you angry or sad or confused? What did it feel like being in your body? Did you feel comfortable with yourself?

Now continue down memory lane... go to grammar school. How did it feel being there? How did you feel about yourself? How did it feel living in the house with your parents? Did you feel safe and secure? Did you feel taken care of or neglected? Did you feel listened to? Did you feel that you were understood? Did you feel loved? How did you feel loved? What did you need to do to feel loved? Did you feel loved for just being the child you were, or did you feel you had to earn your parent's love?

Continue looking in your memory. How did you feel about the way your parents treated each other? Did they treat each other with kindness, respect, and understanding? What did you learn from them about love and togetherness? What did you learn about communication? What did you learn about achieving goals and being strong? What did you learn about the world and how it works? What did you learn about spirituality and the wonders of being alive?

Now, write down some of your feelings in this moment as you answer these questions:

What I learned about being a parent from the way I was parented is…

_____

_____

_____

_____

_____

This is a time of reflection to view how we were conditioned to model or to repeat old patterns with our children. Unless we are able to remove the negative attitudes and beliefs about ourselves, we cannot love someone else unconditionally and expect to accept them as they are. We all make mistakes.

By reflecting on what behaviors we inherited, we can make changes and move on; forgive our parents and forgive ourselves for things we ourselves have done or left undone.

Please breathe and take time to answer this question.

I wish that my parents would have treated me...

_____

_____

_____

Please note that when I speak of positive or negative below, it is not determined by what society deems positive or negative, but rather what feels good, peaceful, and in your best interest of body, mind, and spirit.

As I reflect, I can see that I am repeating the following positive patterns of behavior modeled by my parents...

_____

_____

_____

As I reflect, I can see that I am repeating the following negative patterns of behavior from my parents...

_____

_____

_____

Please be aware also that the way you internalized and experienced the events in your life and how you viewed your parents, siblings, and other family members may not agree with how your parents or others experienced the same events. You are responsible to view and become aware of your own experiences. Whether these were similar to others should not be a measure of your acceptance of your own experiences.

You see, you might have been so loved and so cuddled, that, while it seems like an absolutely wonderful inheritance, it may have made you lethargic, and perhaps you don't have the ability to follow through because when the going gets rough, you give up. Your potential is limitless, but you lack the motivation or the belief or the strength to fulfill your dreams.

Or you might have been in a home that offered you much material wealth and wellbeing and you may not have felt seen, heard or acknowledged for who you are. You may have had parents that were very busy and didn't have time to spend with you. In this case, you might have learned to have goals and aspirations and to focus on a career and success but not on parenting and spending time with your children. Or you might have learned that both are incredibly important and may have been struggling with a need to do it all attitude and couldn't find the balance.

We feel loved when someone wants to spend time with us, when they make the effort to be with us, share with us, listen to us, and see us as valuable.

On the other hand, you might have been brought up by a single mother or father or a grandmother who didn't have much money or education but loved you unconditionally. This is a key component in **Conscious Parenting**. However, we often face issues that prevent us from spending the time we wish or need to dedicate to our children. Let's identify that it is more than the amount of time you spend with your child, it is the quality of time. Even if you were brought up by a single parent who worked many hours, you might have felt that she or he believed in you, and this gave you the confidence and motivation and faith to experience life as full and exciting.

Are You Parenting As Your Parents Parented You?

After you have read these pages, try to look at the ways that you are parenting your children and view the ways that you are "doing the same things your parents did." Are you satisfied with these choices, or would you like to make some adjustments? Write down your thoughts on this.

_____

_____

_____

_____

_____

_____

Now be careful because you also may have sworn that you would never do the same as your parents and you may be going overboard in this endeavor.

Your job as parents is to always do what is in the best interest of your child.

In order to be aware of what is in the best interest of our children at any given moment and keeping at the forefront that we are to develop their already existent potential, we must get out of our own way. We must eliminate our own negative behavior and open ourselves to being present to enter the world of the child.

Now that we have identified these distinct inner voices—the **Inner Parent** and the **Inner Child**—we must also become aware of the inner voice of an effective **Inner Parent**. *That voice represents the voice of a rational caring adult.*

Developing a rational adult in your parenting becomes the voice of reason. The voice that is able to stay in the present and support the **Inner Child** with whatever he or she is dealing with.

Sometimes, however, you will echo what you learned from your parents as the **Inner Parent**. This **Inner Parent** may be critical or immature or rigid. In this case, we must work at changing the internal dialogue so that we can create a firm, rational but loving voice that guides us, and in turn, will be the model that our children emulate.

How to Create a Balanced Inner Parent

The variety of emotions ranging between love/hate through excitement/boredom are exclusive of the **Inner Child**. The voice of the **Inner Parent** cannot dominate and control the emotions of the **Inner Child** through logic and willpower. This causes the **Inner Child** to become resistant and angry. The **Inner Parent** must have the ability to reason with the **Inner Child** by educating them and setting healthy boundaries.

If you observe that you have a strong "critical voice" within yourself, you may experience tremendous inner conversations of resistance or rebellion.

Example: a 42-year-old woman is in a relationship with a man who is very insecure and suspicious. He was abandoned by his mother early in his life and had to fend for himself. He marries unconsciously without really learning about his mate, who gets pregnant within the first month of their relationship. Mary, his wife, a flirtatious and vibrant young woman, made him feel insecure. He then would align himself with negative gossip that he may hear about his wife's flirtatiousness and accuse her of being a cheater. She was not. She received his negative comments as a trigger for her internalized parent that coincided with the message of her real parents who never trusted her. She then reacted to her husband as a rebellious teenager. Instead of reassuring her husband, she became increasingly defensive and became more and more detached and angry. This increased his suspiciousness which made him more accusatory. This triggered his **Inner Child** (I am abandoned) and her **Inner Child** (my parents think I am a bad girl, I'll show them!)

As you go through life and are faced with different choices and experiences, the inner voices of the parent and child will interact within your mind. Frequently, these conversations will be in disagreement. These inner conflicts are often the result of unresolved inner or outer conversations with our parents. If, however, you were brought up in a home where your thoughts and feelings were heard and discussed appropriately, these conflicts will be minimal. It is also true that, if you had no support during these conflicts or your parents were not "mature" and their methods of expression were childish, you may have a great deal of confusion or inability to resolve conflicts.

Please be aware that there must be a healthy balance between your **Inner Parent** and your **Inner Child**, which would be expressed as being a loving and strong guide and a collaborative child. If however, the **Inner Child** is left unchecked, undisciplined or unsupervised, because there is no positive **Inner Parent**, then what could have been a well-balanced person can become an addictive personality. He or she will seek to relieve their anger and frustration with drugs, alcohol, gambling, overeating, sex, or any number of vices. When this happens, the rational conversations of the **Inner Parent** are drowned out by whatever pleasure-seeking activity takes over. The **Inner Child** keeps seeking the calm and nurturing voice of a safe

Inner Parent that does not exist within him via mind-altering substances or experiences.

Whether we are speaking of the internalized **Inner Child** or we are parenting a child, the ideal role is for the child to be itself. This can become very difficult when that child's true voice has been silenced, repressed, ridiculed or punished severely. The **Inner Child** retreats into safety in whatever form it can find it. It is, therefore, extremely difficult to re-parent this **Inner Child** to express his or her feelings after suffering this type of abuse. However, it is never impossible.

Let's take a look at the negative parenting messages of your **Inner Child**:

Were you punished unreasonably because your parents were on edge?

_____

_____

_____

Were you neglected?

_____

_____

_____

Were you abandoned?

_____

_____

_____

Were you overprotected or overindulged?

_____

_____

_____

When you are answering these questions, don't allow yourself to feel like you are betraying your parents. We know that everyone did the best they "knew how" in those moments, and this is why we are interested in the topic of healthy loving parenting. We want to become aware of what we can do that will work better in allowing our children to stay whole and self-expressed as we integrate them into our society.

This **Inner Child** must be made to feel safe again and this is the journey of re-parenting—learning how to ease or replace those negative internal conversations with firm but nurturing conversations that allow you to be yourself and express your wants and needs responsibly.

First of all, you are a unique set of essential physical, emotional, mental, and spiritual characteristics. You were also born at a particular time in life. If you were born in the 50s in India, you would have a cultural codification different from someone born in Indiana during the 70s. More importantly, however, is the fact that you are always your own particular "perceiver" and codify information according to that perception. It is also true that your parents were in a particular mindset or physical state at the time you were born which would have influenced your particular conditioning and how you perceived yourself.

While I always say that none of us are wearing halos or wings, our focus in re-parenting ourselves and in parenting our future generations can be to activate skills that will help us to support, nurture and love ourselves and to further reflect this in our children. This happens when we can accept, teach and empower them to evolve to a separate and distinct self, rather than force them to be a projection of what we would have wished for ourselves or for them.

The most important step to your personal happiness and fulfillment, as well as becoming the best model for parenting, is for you to learn how to Love, Nurture, and Empower your Inner Child, which will then reflect as to how you love, nurture and empower others.

Case History of the Dynamic between Inner Parent and Inner Child

Mary Ann was the oldest of three children. When she was born, her mother was 21 years of age and totally unconscious as a parent and even about herself. As a child, Mary Ann had been emotionally neglected and ridiculed. As a result, her **Inner Child** does not have clear inner parental conversations to help her deal with adverse situations.

When she is faced with confrontation or conflict, she has no internal rational voice to calm her inner child's fears. Her mother was a reaction machine who would scream and cry and feel victimized by her daughter at every turn. Not only did Mary Ann internalize this negative **Inner Parent**, but her **Inner Child** was never re-parented. As a result, her emotional reactions are the same as her mother's used to be. You see, her mother has now done work on herself and is slowly managing to dispel these old behaviors. She mentioned to me in a session, "I see that my daughter is like I was at her age. She gets in such a tizzy, and I can't say anything to her because she is so defensive. It's like she is possessed by a demon." Yes, I thought, she definitely was possessed with the internalized model of that Unconscious Parent that her mother was for her and she mimicked that same behavior to her daughter.

It is so important for all of us to reflect deeply and to re-parent ourselves. Otherwise, what is running our present moment is nothing more than the unconscious **internalized messages** which become our self-parenting guidance.

Until you become conscious of yourself, you are nothing more than a robot carrying out a model of being that was programmed in you.

Creating A Healthy Inner Parent And A Collaborative Inner Child

We seldom experience conflicts when both the **Inner Parent** and the **Inner Child** are satisfied. This means that they are both feeling in harmony with themselves and each other. The **Inner Parent** is getting what it needs and so is the **Inner Child**. This is exactly what we aim for in parenting our own children, right? We want them to collaborate with us. However, problems arise when one of the selves goes into conflict. The most important thing to learn is how to resolve these inner conflicts.

How to Resolve These Inner Conflicts

The **Inner Parent** must always be in charge and aware of what is happening to the **Inner Child**. When there is conflict, you will experience confusion, indecision, or a constant heated inner conversation that does not get resolved. You are having an inner argument.

The **Inner Parent** must recognize that there is a conflict.

The **Inner Parent** must have accumulated the emotional maturity to be able to step away and look for a solution where there is a win/win possibility. Often, there is no rational or centered **Inner Parent**. Some people are Inner Orphans, meaning their **Inner Parent** is not helpful because it was internalized as a wounded and irrational parent, in which case the **Inner Child** feels like it cannot find a solution and gets more resistant or angry or annoyed and depressed.

Until you can distance yourself from a situation automatically, it is valuable to write down the needs or desires of each of the internal conversations.

It is then up to the rational you to try to find possible solutions to this internal dilemma by listening attentively and without judgment to these needs.

Once you have listened to the needs within you, which may be displayed by the conflicting inner conversations, you try to find possible solutions. A good way to do this is to make lists. You will find that the **Inner Child** may want immediate action while the **Inner Parent** may be more apprehensive to make changes.

The **Inner Child** and **Inner Parent** find a solution to a given situation.

The **Inner Child** and **Inner Parent** put into action the solution.

Both the **Inner Child** and the **Inner Parent** evaluate and talk about their solution and discuss what could be changed or adjusted. This creates a cooperative interaction between the **Inner Child** and a rational caring **Inner Parent**.

Please observe that as you are able to create this balance within yourself, you will naturally use the same methods for effective parenting with your children to resolve conflicts. These steps are essential to follow as your children move from pre-adolescence to their teens. Otherwise, you will undoubtedly have very high levels of resistance.

I am sharing this personal experience with you to bring to light how a child makes decisions very early in life and how when we are unconscious as parents, we never even detect that our children are internalizing some very negative conversations. Below is a personal example of how a **Conscious Parent** can listen to a child and interrupt a decision that could negatively affect his or her development.

> *I remember an incident that happened during the time that my son's father and I were separated. His father moved about three blocks away from our family home. My son was just 6 years of age and very close to his*

father and me. He had lived a very safe life and had not been involved in any arguing or dramatic events during his early years until his father and I decided not to be together. Even then, we were both strongly committed to being there for our son.

My son's dad had moved into his apartment and my son went over to visit his father. I remember calling his house and my son answered. I said, "Hi, Mommy will be coming to pick you up in a few minutes." He said "okay" and seemed cheerful. However, when his father brought him to the car, he was crying and very emotional. As soon as my son was in the car, he began to get very nervous and almost frantic, saying, "Mommy, please I have to go home and get my pajamas. I have to come back and stay with my Daddy." I remember how heart-wrenching it was to see him begin to cry uncontrollably, as if it was his responsibility to save his father and make him feel okay. We stopped in front of the house, and I remember holding him and trying to calm him down. As he was weeping, he said, "My life will never work out." I heard him, and I was at first shocked that a child so small could make such a statement. This was clear evidence that all of us, when we were faced with traumatic moments in our early years, made decisions about what occurred that became the pivot from which we then created our identity in the world.

As I was fully present to him as a **Conscious Parent,** I heard this inner decision in time to help him interrupt it before the decision became a constant inner conversation for his life.

I said quickly. "No, that is not true, your life is going to be wonderful. Daddy is okay and so is Mommy. We both love you very much and you are safe no matter where Mommy and Daddy live. We are always with you, and you don't need to ever worry about that." I kept repeating, "You are safe, you are safe." I took him inside the house, and I held him for what seemed like hours until he fell asleep."

Our children will inevitably model the way they were parented. I assert that by reparenting ourselves and becoming **Conscious Parents**, our children will internalize a new listening and behaviors that will interrupt any negative inner voice and replace it with a clear rational caring voice.

As I became a **Conscious Parent**, I was able to reparent myself and create within a rational caring **Inner Parent** and a collaborative **Inner Child**. This gave me the ability to parent and empower my son so that he inherited this healthy rational **Inner Parent** and collaborative **Inner Child**. While I was unconscious in parenting my daughter, this new internalized parent and collaborative child allowed me to create a wonderful and loving relationship with my daughter as she grew into adulthood.

Healing Our Relationships With Our Partners/Co-Parents/Caregivers

W hether you are in a marriage, living with a partner, living separately, raising your children with a relative, a nanny, or are divorced or widowed, you still have either an active or inactive relationship with the child's other parent or guardian. You have either a loving or an indifferent, numb, conflicted, and inconsistent relationship. Your relationship with the individual who is raising your children with you must be reviewed. You must make sure that you are co-parenting in a way that assures your child is receiving words and actions from caregivers that are not contradictory. Children learn from what we do more than from what we say.

You must be willing to take the same action in your relationship with the individual with whom you are raising your children as you did when you reviewed and revised your relationship to yourself. The attitudes and choices that you make reflect a foundation of respect for yourself and for your children. You are the model for the kind of love and respect that your children will feel that they deserve in a relationship with a mate as they grow older, as well as for the way they will communicate and how they will resolve their conflicts.

Few of us have the gift of innate communication skills or conflict resolution tools.

I'll tell couples with children: Creating a family is not JUST about you! When you choose to marry and then bring children into the world, you are no longer thinking singularly. It is about how you are going to make the necessary adjustments in your life so that you can be guardians of your child's precious life. You must always think, and I reiterate: ***What is in the best interest of our child?*** And this does not always mean that it is possible to stay together. If you don't know how to communicate respectfully, then you must learn. If you don't know how to be a responsible and loving parent, you must learn to become one. Whether or not you continue to live with the child's biological parent, you will always be your child's parent. I have heard a number of individuals say to me, "I realize what a commitment it is to have children and so I have chosen not to have them." Well, that is fair enough. This is how being conscious works—you reflect on the action and the consequences that this action would present and then you make a conscious decision.

A strong, loving, and working relationship will be the cornerstone for the "safe space" which will be created to bring children into the world. I will speak more about the safe space in a later chapter. For now, the safe space entails security, respect, love, and forgiveness.

Guidelines to Collaborative Parenting

Talk often. Discuss your parenting philosophies. Discuss how you were parented and discuss how you want to implement/avoid similar measures. Speak gently but be clear about your thoughts and boundaries.

Come to agreements about house rules, punishments, and important family values (culture, religion, etc.) Coming to firm agreements that both parties are comfortable with will eliminate resentment. Agree to talk again to add new agreements when necessary.

Present a united front in the presence of your child. Step away to discuss further in private if necessary and return only when a clear conclusion has been drawn.

Case Study - How Conscious Are Our Relationship Choices, Values, and Beliefs?

I remember when I got a call from a concerned 34-year-old man who wanted desperately to make an appointment for couples counseling. He said that he and his wife were going through a lot of difficulties. They came together for the first session and each one began to reveal what their particular story was.

Cindy and Michael met in a club and felt instantly attracted to each other. They spent almost every day together after that. This was approximately 10 years before they came to see me. Cindy was divorced and was enjoying herself and she didn't know that Michael had been in a four-year long-distance relationship, which he was finding hard to maintain. Although he had been committed and faithful to his girlfriend for all those years, he was unconsciously or consciously looking for someone to hold. He met Cindy and it was great. They both got caught in the spell of infatuation and lust and had unprotected sex. After six weeks, she told Michael that she was pregnant. He was already having doubts about his four-year relationship and was trying to decide what to do. She tells Michael that she will not think of not having the child— she will have the child and, if he does not want to be part of the child's life, then that is okay with her. In other words, she made the decision and gave him no choice. He wanted to do the right thing and, being caught up in the spell of lust, decided that they should get married. They married and, during the pregnancy, they were still feeling good together until family members and friends in the town started gossiping and telling Michael that she had been dating before they got together. They made him doubt as to whether or not their precious little girl was indeed his. In the midst of what should be the foundation of the **Safe Space** needed for a workable marriage and pregnancy, they were both facing suspicion, fear, and anxieties. After a paternity test, it was clear that Michael was the father of their daughter Olivia.

When they began to unravel the web of insecurities with this lack of understanding between infatuation or chemical attraction and responsibly choosing a mate, it became clear that their initial encounter was not ready for a lifetime commitment. They had not created a safe space for trust and, if they both really were now committed to learning to know and love each other, they stood a great chance of creating a healthy and loving relationship. While they both had a lack of safe parenting, these issues can be overturned through expert psychotherapy and counseling if there is a commitment and desire to work together. They did work on their relationship and reconnected to the love they felt for each other, which was greater than the obstacles, and learned how to communicate, let go of their resentments, and find ways to negotiate their differences.

We sometimes choose our partners unconsciously.

I know that there are many of you reading this who were more conscious. Perhaps you even wrote your own vows, and you have done your best to carry them out. What I am saying is that we did not, for the most part, have the education to know what it takes to have a successful marriage.

When we choose a partner in life in an unconscious way, we don't take time to think about who the person we are marrying or having children with is. Is this person who I am attracted to and feel a connection with really ready, willing, and able to take on the responsibility of marriage and parenting?

We look at relationships primarily from the emotional level of "I find this person attractive." We are drawn to each other chemically and we begin a relationship without thinking ahead. We must realize that there are more ingredients necessary for a successful partnership than physical chemistry. We must be able to make the distinction between looking for love and looking for a loving partner. In my therapeutic experience, men are a bit clearer between chemistry or sexual attraction and love than women. By this, I mean that men are usually conditioned to make a distinction between sex and love. However, it is also true that men can be misled by this chemistry to give in to a woman's wants without really thinking of the consequences. It seems that, if the romance is going well, then we stay together in the daze or spell of "falling in love." We don't pay attention to what in the long term will constitute the foundation for a strong and healthy working relationship.

Observing Your Relationship

I don't know how old you are or what your particular background is. What I do know, after speaking with thousands of people both young and past 50, is that we did not actively learn to be in a healthy relationship. For the most part, we carried on imitating what we learned from our parents and society at the time we got into a relationship.

Take a few moments and write down any similarities in the way you are living your life that resembles that of your parents. If it works for you, keep it in. If it does not, be willing to take action to change.

Consider the following questions:

How did your parents show their love to one another or lack of it?

_____

_____

_____

How did they resolve problems? Did they do this together?

_____

_____

_____

How did they communicate?

_____

_____

_____

How did they meet?

_____

_____

_____

Did they enjoy each other? Did they laugh?

_____

_____

_____

Dee's Story - Healing My Relationship with My Father Changed My View of Men

I didn't know or meet my biological father until I was 26 years old when I went to live in Buenos Aires, Argentina. My mother was at a singing engagement when the wife of my father's cousin went to visit my mother and gave her a phone number. My mother gave the number to me. I called Pocha (that was her nickname). She wanted to see me and so I went to her house and met my second cousins. I also met my father's children since they would go to Pocha's for lunch almost every day. They didn't know I was their step-sister. We ate together and related on a surface level while I waited for my cousin to tell my father that I wanted to meet him. A couple of months passed and still, I didn't have a specific date to see my father. I heard where he might be working and that he did want to see me.

It was a bright sunny day when I left my apartment and an intuitive voice within me said, "Today is the day — go find your father." I got into a taxi and directed it towards the area where I thought my father was working. I got out of the car and almost within the first five minutes I entered a store and I saw my cousin walking towards me with a man with grey hair and bright blue eyes who introduced himself to me. He said, "Te conozco hace mucho tiempo." In Spanish, this means, "I've known you for a long time." I remember being mildly shocked and more concerned with how he might be feeling than with my own feelings. We sat in a coffee shop for about an hour and talked about him and my mother. I remember getting together with him at another time and then we never saw each other again. I heard some years later that he passed away.

Ten years ago, when I participated in self-development training, I got in touch with my buried feelings about this man who I really never knew but whose DNA was a gift to me. I realized that having an absent father had given me internal conversations not only about the characteristics of a father but also of the men that I would seek out.

My father was not there, not available to me in any way. He was absent. I know that I had substitutes for him in my grandfather who was definitely present and my uncles, but they also became inaccessible to me when I was taken to live in the United States. What was consistent for me is that men in my life could not be relied upon. I created an idea inside that sooner or later they would leave or be taken away. It has taken me a great deal of inner work to try to dissolve the impact of these conversations and to substitute them for healthier ones that say, "You are lovable and it is wonderful for someone to take care of you." "You can trust a man. There are men who will not let you down." "You can learn to distinguish what is right and good for you."

I grew up without trusting that I would be protected and supported or loved unconditionally by a man. This has been the toughest inner conversation to change. It was finally in 1998 when I participated in a remarkable and powerful training program in New York City that I got in touch fully with my inner unresolved conversations about my absent father. I wrote a letter to him that I still have, and, in the letter, I spoke about the ways that I had made him wrong.

"...I saw you through the eyes of not good enough and that is the way I would eventually see every man that I was with... my perception about men was that they would not be there for me..."

It was then that I began to see men with more understanding and compassion. My negative view slowly began to be replaced by one of viewing men as "enough" and I felt gratitude for what men go through and contribute to our lives. This healing allowed me to create an extraordinary safe space for men in couples counseling and support women to correct their cast iron viewpoints of either what a man should be or what a man could never be.

My internalized mother image was not much more consistent. As I mentioned before, my mother had no time for me. She was a world-renowned opera singer and that was her primary focus until she later gave birth to my brother, Peter, with her second husband. She was this make-believe person to me whom I admired from afar. I saw her in beautiful gowns on the stage, while my grandmother and my aunt Nata, my mother's sister, did most of the daily nurturing. I was definitely nurtured by them, and so I internalized mothering and being loved by women who made me safe and accepted me but thought that they would eventually leave me. I realized later that I was always open when I met a new friend with whom I felt comfortable. However, in the back of my mind, I would be apprehensive as to how safe or relaxed I could feel. I would automatically be open at first, but then a fear would come in to replace my open heart. This fear would then transform me into a more reserved and suspicious person.

My mother and father did not provide me with the support or unconditional safe space that I needed, but I am proud to have been able to forgive them for what they were not able to give me, and, instead of disowning them, I am able to integrate their positive qualities in myself. I have alternatively managed to create an inner loving parent. The process of re-parenting myself has allowed me to create an inner reliable prosthesis to compensate for a void of consistent parental support. New positive internal conversations hold little Dee with love, support, and empowerment. My fears of abandonment are no longer at the forefront of my existence and I really know that there is someone, besides a higher power, that will be an unshakeable foundation. It is this very resourceful and fun-loving part of me that I share with so many people. I take good care of myself and I don't have a need to find people to fill a void in me. I feel whole and complete, even when I am alone.

We often prefer to remain unconscious in order to pursue the pleasure that we get temporarily without thinking of the long-term consequences. Our children receive our unconscious patterns. Some of the ingredients that set the foundation for a truly safe space in a relationship are:

- Emotional maturity - having the ability to balance your feelings and an objective view of any given situation. This encompasses an ability to not take everything personally and to listen and respect another's point of view, even when you don't agree with it.

- The ability to communicate your needs and your wants clearly.

- A similar ethical vision of life. This does not mean, "We like the same movies and the same food." It means that what we both want to create and live out individually and as a couple in this lifetime is congruent. We are feeling and thinking in the same direction.

- A spiritual awareness that is practiced in daily life to assure a connectedness when trials and tribulations are thrown in our path.

Much of what will prepare us to become **Conscious Parents** is the willingness to ponder all of these matters. You might say, "Well, I didn't think about these things and I have been unconscious and I did marry unconsciously. I now realize that I didn't have the tools to make choices that were really in my best interest, but here I am. What do I do now?" The answer is: You become conscious now! It is not about criticizing yourself, nor thinking that you have to change your partner or feel tremendous guilt for what you didn't do before, although you might feel it. If you do, it is natural, but try to keep from criticizing yourself for the past. We all have done the best we knew how at each moment in our lives. Life is for learning and growing in awareness. At each stage of our development, we experience things according to our awareness at that time. If we had been in a different mindset, perhaps many of us would not have constructed a wall of fear instead of an opening to love.

When I reflect on this statement after nine years of marriage to my son's father and a divorce, I feel that the ingredients for a successful marriage were present in each of us as potential, but certainly were not actualized. We liked each other and enjoyed each other's company. We superficially liked similar things. I remember how excited we were because we liked the same food and the same movies. However, we were lacking the skills to be good communicators and to resolve conflict. When we faced a challenge, we would begin to argue. This led to us either giving in and resenting one another or giving in and withdrawing our love. Certainly, the main component of really being present and listening to each other was missing.

This is where many couples get stuck. We are all good with the fun stuff, but the real challenge of marriage is the part of the vows that says, "For better or for worse, in sickness or in health." How do we deal with conflict resolution and with our differences?

What Works

The lesson here is to know when you are feeling disappointed and to try to find a solution that works for both of you. It is not about hoping that you will never have challenges because that would be unrealistic. It is, however, about acquiring the tools that can help heighten communication and conflict resolution. Learning to use these tools is one of the most important factors in a loving relationship. When you feel disappointed, hurt, frustrated, or angry with your partner, you must find a way to speak out and express what you feel and what you need without being reactive. Obviously, this is a skill that needs training.

It is crucial in all relationships to know how to set boundaries for yourself and with others. There is a difference between venting your feelings and thoughts and really communicating what is really there. Communicate what you want instead of being accusatory. Ask, "What is your experience?" When you communicate, make it about you. When you communicate, you look within your own heart and say what you need and want without making the other person wrong. Example: You feel alone or need attention or affection from the other person. Instead of, "You never give me a hug, or you don't spend time with me," say, "I miss being close to you. I need some of your affection." Then have a conversation as to how to create that together.

Cultivate a strong friendship with your mate. My ex-husband's father said something very important to him when he told his father that he and I were going to be married. He said, "I know you love her, but do you like her?" Even when I am sure that at the time my ex did like me, I thought it was an insulting remark because it seemed like they did not approve of me for reasons that I did not find justifiable. However, after many years of growth and reflection, I understand what he was saying. We often feel in love or attracted, but we don't necessarily stop to think if we really like each other enough to withstand the challenges that the commitment to being together requires. If there was no sex, no money, nothing but the two of us, would we still feel that he or she is my best friend? Is this the person that I would choose to partner with through thick and thin? What his father was saying in retrospect was, "Are you both sure that you can partner together successfully and that you have enough things in common so that your differences won't outweigh your similarities?" I also understand, without any judgment, that we can grow apart, not from lack of similarities but from eventually wanting to travel a road that the other is not committed to.

Ingredients Necessary for Successful, Long Term, Loving Relationships

A connection of the heart. This is the magical feeling that we get when we feel attracted to someone. You feel chemistry and connection not only on a physical level but on a mental and emotional level as well. You enjoy who they are being. You accept each other exactly the way you are.

Similarities of interests, values, dreams, and ambitions. It is especially powerful when a couple creates a vision that they are both invested in realizing, not a goal, but a commitment to something bigger than living daily life. Perhaps they create a contribution to a cause that the couple will try to fulfill together. This keeps them aligned with each other.

The ability to communicate easily and respectfully. Communication cannot occur without the following elements:

- Successful listening

- Staying present with one another

- The ability to stay open emotionally to another person

- The capability not to get defensive

- A desire and ability to focus on solutions instead of staying stuck on the problem

A deep trust, which is the cornerstone to love. Trust grows as we get to know and understand our differences. If an ability to converse and discuss issues is not available in the relationship, then assumptions and interpretations are made according to each individual. Conflicts are not resolved. Hurt feelings become internalized. This buildup of resentment creates walls to our trust and love.

We may never meet the "perfect" person who will agree with everything we want or think. Differences are a great asset when we are able to understand them and use them to expand the partnership.

Example: Mary is a very outgoing person and makes friends easily. John is a very detailed person who does not feel comfortable socializing with a large number of people.

If John and Mary do not discuss these differences and find a solution that works for both of them, they will use their differences to separate from each other. On the other hand, if they discuss their differences, they may be able to find ways to use them as assets rather than liabilities while recognizing and respecting each other's differences. Maybe Mary would go out once a week with her friends, but, when they socialize together, it will be in small groups.

The ability to feel unconditionally safe with your partner. This means that there is nothing that you cannot discuss with your partner, even if it is difficult to do so. You or your partner may find it difficult to accept behaviors or decisions that are made. However, he or she is there for the long haul.

I heard something which resonated with me for a long time. The person said, "Great marriages are made by great forgivers," the opposite of this being "great fault finders." I believe that most of us fall in "conditional love." As soon as there is a characteristic or incident in which either person falls short of our ideal, we judge them and hold it against them. This does not work. There has to be an acceptance that problems will always arise. The challenge is to grow our ability to resolve them. To feel safe with someone, you must be provided with an opportunity to speak and have your voice and point of view heard, even when the person may not agree with you. We feel safe when we are not criticized. The individual is more interested in learning about what you feel and think than trying to impose their agenda on you.

Lack of conflict resolution skills. When I work with couples, I can always detect when they started building the walls of separation to their love, as I call them. When did they first feel a great disappointment in the other? If they create walls of fear, they can eventually block the love from our hearts.

Spiritual Healing

A parent who develops Spiritual Attunement is better able to see, hear, and acknowledge their child.

Regardless of your religious inclination or beliefs, developing your spiritual body is essential for a parent to really learn to trust their own instincts and connect to their child. We are constantly trying to figure out what we need to do with our children because we have not explored or developed our instincts and intuition. When you are tuned in to your spiritual self, you are in a constant state of alertness. You observe and question the ways that you think and act. Why? Because you are tuned in to a higher listening or viewing of yourself and others than just that of your society or the collective consciousness of the community that you were born into or choose to live in.

You are tuned in to a power greater than your physical existence. In so doing, you begin to develop a sixth sense or a multidimensional sense of reality. You utilize all of your senses to become aware of a power within you which gives unlimited guidance. This intuitive intelligence expands your ability to view your child, or children, without preconceptions. This allows the parent to practice patience with their child because, while the parent is dealing with the everyday routines of living, they are aware of taking the time for what is essential in their relationship with their child. The chores, homework, laundry, etc. is never more important than being with, acknowledging, or listening to your child. Life has a deeper meaning. The most important thing we can give each other is our ability to be fully present. The parent never loses sight of instilling values and social rules in raising their children— they include their intuitive intelligence in making choices and decisions that affect the wellbeing of the whole family. The spiritual understanding of the interconnectedness of all life allows for decisions to be made not on what is just good for one but rather what is in the best interest of all.

You may use prayer and meditation as a tool to commune with this creative force and put what you need in the hands of the universal intelligence. If you have developed spiritually, you will have learned to read the signs or the messages that this inner guidance sends to you. You, therefore, become more confident in your ability to parent and less concerned with trying to be "the parent that society may deem acceptable at the time."

When you are using this spiritual guidance, your choices can be almost diametrically opposed to what may seem logical to your society, but you follow them because you have developed an instinct that trusts your inner guidance. It is this added element to who you are that assists you in being able to give your child the fundamental ingredient to grow emotionally whole. Trusting our inner guidance as parents gives our children that element so that they in turn feel seen, heard, and acknowledged. This is the mirror we all need to grow.

When you are seen by another, you are reflected back in your true self. Your unlimited potential is viewed by the parent. This feedback empowers a child to feel that his or her presence is valuable and unique. When you are heard or listened to, you internalize a sense that your voice is heard, and it makes a difference. Finally, we all need to feel acknowledged for what we do and the contribution that we make.

> ### Summary- Healing Our Relationships With Our Partners/Co-Parents/Caregivers
>
> Co-create means that together you intentionally invent the environment you want.

Mate responsibly and do the inner work to make the difference. Discuss and create a workable outcome.

Observe your relationship. Regularly evaluate the health of the relationship. Take actionable steps to improve upon trouble spots.

Find a solution. Don't pass on unconscious patterns. Don't step over unconscious patterns in the relationship. Know when you're disappointed, communicate and find a solution that works for both of you.

Ingredients for a successful relationship.

 A connection of the heart

 Similar interests, values, dreams, ambitions

 The ability to communicate easily and respectfully

 A deep trust, which is the cornerstone to love

A parent who develops Spiritual Attunement is better able to see, hear, and acknowledge their child.

PART IV:

LISTENING WITH THE HEART

Our practice in parenting has not been to see our children as bearing gifts for us to discover and co-create with them. They are not only a gift to us, but also to life. Our job is to support their development of self-confidence, self-trust, and self-expression. We must give them room so that they can express their thoughts and feelings appropriately in the world. We must clarify for ourselves that teaching our children is not defined as a way of being that seeks to "make an individual better" or to "make them into our expectations." As we observe them, we can see that they may bring certain talents and we can then open doors for these talents to be nurtured. This is the gateway to rearing self-reliant, collaborative, actualized future citizens.

How Do You Become A Listener Of The Heart?

You have already worked on re-parenting yourself and creating a working relationship with your spouse, caregivers, and teachers so that you are all aligned in the basic philosophy. While becoming aware of authenticity and learning to make conscious choices is a long-term unfolding venture, I hope that you have taken the time to do an evaluation of how you are healing yourself. You have also been led through taking an inventory as to how you are relating to your partner or other significant caregivers and hopefully are learning new ways of communication, conflict resolution, and setting boundaries. You are now ready to learn how to parent consciously as a **Listener Of The Heart**.

Practices of Listening With The Heart

I have outlined eleven practices for *Listening With The Heart* that have served me and many other parents who struggled to communicate with their children in ways that promote actualization. These practices are:

Creating a Safe Space for Your Children

Discovering, Uncovering, and Empowering Your Children's Potential

Being Present and Listening to Your Child

Communicating Effectively

Withholding Judgement and Criticism

Being Authentic With Your Children

Giving Your Children Choices from a Young Age

Entrusting Your Children to Collaborate

Managing Resistance in Your Children

Empowering Your Children to Listen to the Answers Within

Dealing With Your Children as they Reach Adolescence

These practices are the keys to maintaining a child whole and complete throughout the stages of their development.

Creating a Safe Space for Your Children

I sat one day with a cup of coffee early on a summer's morning and pondered this question: *Why is it that family is so important?* I had the insight that family is meant to be our safe space. In a world of differences and contradictions, family is to be the one place where we truly feel safe. Safe means that I can be myself fully. I have an unconditional place of acceptance. This is a place within me and outside of me that I can go back to anytime and know that whatever the issues may be, I am welcomed, accepted, and supported. I am unconditionally loved.

Wow, I thought, how many individuals have really experienced this kind of love? So, I filled another cup of coffee and thought some more. Does unconditionally loving someone mean that I like everything that my child does? Does it mean that I do not correct my child when he or she steps over the guidelines for respecting themselves or others? The answer is NO. I assert that I need to discover and accept my child's potential and keep that at the forefront of parenting while I give him or her the skills to fit into society. This is different entirely than forcing him or her into society's expectations. The distinction here is that we teach them to follow the guidelines of our society by first modeling these guidelines and secondly by showing them how to act in the world in a way that does not shame, criticize, or punish them for their self-expression and creativity.

To hold a safe space for our children or anyone in our lives means that we:

- Accept and love the other unconditionally

- Don't have to agree with them

- Suspend being judgmental

- Try to access their point of view with compassion

- Have clear boundaries about what we need and want and are able to express and stand firm in them

While this is true for any relationship, it is especially important when raising healthy, self-reliant, and cooperative young people.

Reflections on My Own Safe Space

I know when I look back on my childhood, I had a safe space with my grandparents for my first 6 years of life— safe in the sense that I knew I was loved by them and that they accepted and even celebrated who I was. However, as I grew up, my grandparents went far away, and I was put in a boarding school, my safe space was gone forever. I mention this fact because as children we develop our self-esteem from the way that we are treated and by how consistent we feel our guardians and caregivers are in their actions and commitment to us.

While my safe space was unconditional with my grandparents, their sudden departure when they returned to Argentina with no explanation as to where they were or why they were gone, created anxiety within me. I was left and had no explanation for their departure. I made up my own reason. At the age of seven, I felt that I must have done something wrong and was bad or they would not have gone away.

My caregivers were replaced from these unconditionally loving grandparents to nuns in a boarding school with rigid rules, an absent stepfather, and a mother who was too busy to be with me or pay attention to me. These last two people, being very significant, didn't seem to recognize me at all. It was in this way that I began to internally weave what I term a split safe space.

On the one hand, I was safe inside my inherited view of myself from my grandparents as being unconditionally loved. I was free to be. I was free to express myself, I was free to explore. The split happened when I lost them and that safety of being loved was replaced by inner conversations of fear, doubt and distrust of all people who were close to me. I experienced this split over and over in my life and in most of my adult relationships. What do I mean? I mean that initially when I met someone, I would view them through the eyes of my grandparents love and give myself fully only to then feel shocked when they didn't show up in this ideal of unconditional love that I learned to expect from my grandparents. It was at this point that I would withdraw, close down and feel alone; the same way I felt when I was put in the boarding school. I would trust unconditionally and open myself and believe what was being offered and being said to me was truthful and I would believe it all without questioning. I would be like a little child who wanted to believe in fairy tales, only to then feel disappointed or betrayed because those same people would not be there to love me unconditionally, which was what I anticipated.

Now, as I look back on the safe space that my grandparents provided for me, it was an unconditional space of love and acceptance, but they did not teach me to have healthy boundaries. Setting boundaries is necessary for people to know where they begin and end and where others start. I, like many of us, believed that what I saw and felt must obviously be what others saw and felt. I have had to remind myself and others in my psychotherapeutic practice that, "Other people don't walk around with our views. They have developed their own set of conditioning and codification." Oh, NO! However, it was a very valuable revelation when, through my inner healing work, I came to understand and practice setting boundaries for myself. My grandparents accepted me unconditionally, perhaps sometimes even to their own detriment. While getting my own way felt good, it did not teach me that others are different and that I need to be aware of the differences. It also did not teach me that what I felt, or thought was not what the other person felt or thought.

Discovering, Uncovering, and Empowering Your Children's Potential

I suggest that you take a few hours to be with your child and really "be present" and observe what they say and do. Become aware of what she or he enjoys and dislikes. First, do this without commenting. If you want to have a dialogue, ask questions and, most of all hear with your heart and listen attentively to gather information. Do this for one week and write down what you discover about your child. Of course, you may discover things that you may not approve of. This exercise is not about you, it is about being observant of your child. It is not to judge your child.

An example of written observations:

> I observed that Melissa is slow-moving. She is quiet and really likes her crayons, especially the color red. She talks with her bear and treats it the same way that I treat her. Sometimes she is rough with her bear...

If you have an older child, do this exercise and just "be with" your son or daughter. Observe what he or she likes doing. Do not make comments. I had a client say to me, "I wanted my child to be an achiever like me, but she is more introspective and enjoys taking her time and contemplating nature." Then she added, "I am disappointed because she does not excel at school. It makes me feel like a failure. I want her to do well in the world. It reminds me of how I used to be at school."

I suggested that she still needed to clear some of her past. She was trying to fix herself as a child by wanting her own child to be what she felt she should have been. If I had not pointed this out to her, she would have tried and tried to make her daughter into her idealized version, in this way destroying what was already natural for her daughter and not discovering this potential.

I reminded her that her job is to be a guardian for her child and that as a guardian the child doesn't belong to her. Kahlil Gibran, the Lebanese poet and prophet, said, "They come from a place we have not yet discovered." Our children come into this world, and we have a hand in nurturing this life intrauterine, but, while we are given the job of nurturing and developing life, we are the custodians of our children. As we are able to be with our children and observe them and discover their gifts, we can then open doors for them so that they can fulfill their potential while they are here on Earth. If we just want to fulfill our own expectations, we interfere with their already coded potential and displace their possible contribution. It is clear that your children will be influenced by you in all ways possible, but you want to give them space to "discover" themselves. You can only do this when you observe who your children are, instead of what you wish them to be.

Being Present and Listening to Your Child

L istening to your children with the heart is a distinct way of being with your children. First, let's distinguish hearing from listening. Webster's definition of "hearing" is the process, function, or power of perceiving sound. Earshot.

Before I go further by distinguishing listening, I want to emphasize the tremendous importance as children and adults of being heard. We despair in life because we are not heard and thus feel misunderstood and alone.

"Listening" is the ability to accurately receive and interpret messages in the communication process. Without the ability to listen effectively, messages can be easily misunderstood.

Listening happens when you give the speaker your undivided attention and acknowledge the message. You acknowledge the message by clearly repeating what was said. Also acknowledge any non-verbal communication. Look at the speaker directly and put aside any distractions. Being present is one of the most difficult ways to be in life and, of course, it may be severely lacking with our children. Notice for yourself. We are always in thought. It is what we do as human beings. We think we are present because we hear with our ears what is being said. I suggest that you really pay attention to your ability to be right where you are when you are with your children. Notice when you are thinking about what to say or the next thing you have to do. I also suggest that you take courses, if possible, in any discipline that will help you be in the present moment.

Listening Practices:

Identify the moment you are in. "I am sitting here. I said I was going to read to my child."

Make being mindful a practice.

Listen without intending to respond. Breathe when you are eager to respond or interrupt. Slow yourself down.

Be okay with not knowing all the answers.

Notice and feel your feelings.

Practice silence at least once a day for 5 minutes and then increase the time in your practice.

Reduce distractions.

These practices are not only for a better connection with your children but work in every area of your life.

Additionally, some guidelines to listening with your child:

First, I suggest that you take a moment and get present in your heart your love for your child. It may require some time to close your eyes and decompress. Once you are present, then be with your child.

Here is a practice:

Pay attention, no interruptions.

Withhold any judgment.

Take a few moments to reflect on what was said.

Clarify anything you didn't hear or understand.

Summarize what was said.

Be aware so that you can put yourself in the shoes of the child according to their age and unique ways of being. Think back to when you were that age.

And finally, some thoughts on giving feedback to your child:

> Do not talk AT your child.
>
> Resonate with their feelings and empathize.
>
> Share what you can remember feeling and doing at that age.
>
> Give advice after you and your child have done the above without making anything wrong.

An example of a conversation between parent and child that you should avoid.

The child comes home and says:

> CHILD (age between 8-10): Somebody stole my new pen.
>
> MOTHER: Are you sure you didn't lose it?

C: *I didn't, it was on my desk when I went to the bathroom.*

M: *You've had things taken before. I always tell you to keep your things inside your desk if you aren't there. The trouble is that you never listen.*

C: *You don't understand.*

M: *Don't talk back to me.*

Instead, try this:

CHILD: *Somebody stole my new pen.*

MOTHER: *Oh no!*

C: *I left it on my desk when I went to the bathroom and somebody took it.*

M: *Mmm...*

C: *This is the third time I have had my pen stolen.*

M: *Uhhh...*

C: I know from now on when I leave the room that I'm going to hide my pen in my desk.

M: I see, great idea.

Listening to Your Child's Feelings

Some quick guidelines:

> Listen with full attention.
>
> Acknowledge their feelings with words like, "Oh, I see…"
>
> Give their feelings a name (i.e. "I know it makes you sad," etc.)
>
> If they have a fantasy of wanting to hurt or express anger towards themselves or someone else, be willing to listen those feelings. Example: "You are so angry that you want to go and hit Nancy, right?"

Listening is not just hearing what he or she says, it is a function of observation and asking distinct questions. The questions are meant for you to discover your child as well as to give him or her a voice.

You want to know how they view the world and how it makes them feel? Here are some questions. If you can, begin these questions from the time they can speak. Add questions that you can think of that invite curiosity.

What is important to you?

Do you think that animals can talk?

Do you like the wind and the sun?

Why do you like to play?

What do you like about school?

What makes you feel good?

What makes you feel bad?

What do you think is nice about you?

Why do people have friends?

Posing simple philosophical questions to your child has them explore their own views.

The constant discovery of a child's potential and desires may prompt the parent to open doors for them. These may be in sports, education, or in their emotional and personal interactions. Discovering your child's interests and potential prompts you to point them in a direction where they can practice discovering those talents in the world.

When you are planning things in the home or with your family, even when you think they don't know or understand, ask them questions so that they are always included in the process of living. You are sourcing their creativity and self-expression. You are also validating their worth.

After the age of 3, ask them to participate in the home. Example: Mommy is so thirsty; can you bring me a cup of water? If your child doesn't know how to get it, show them. Delight when they are able to give you water. It will make your child feel valued and competent.

Some Thoughts on Discipline

The old model for discipline was to punish your children. Punishing your child makes you as the parent the enemy to hide from, instead of the safe space to turn to for support. Being yelled at numbs a child's ability to hear and to listen.

Ways to teach discipline to your children:

Point out ways to be helpful.

Express strong disapproval without attacking the child's character.

State your expectation.

Show the child how to make amends.

Give a choice.

Take action.

Allow the child to experience the consequences of his or her behavior.

Communicating Effectively

Through resonating or empathizing with your child's feelings and thoughts, you are able to access your child's inner world and open a bridge to that world with compassion and understanding. Recreate what the child is saying – reflect back so that they know they are being heard. It is in this way that you create a connection with your child. As you are in connection, there is a mutual listening that is grounded in respect and love. This foundation creates a safe space for the parent to transmit information and educate their child, but most importantly for the information to be received and assimilated by the child. This is what I call **Co-Creating** with your child.

How do we do this?

Resonate with instead of "talking at" your child.

Don't interrupt, correct what he is saying while the child is speaking. Make suggestions after the child has been heard.

An example of how one can achieve this:

Child: Mommy I don't want to go to the doctor.

Unconscious Parent: You have to go to the doctor; all children go to the doctor.

Conscious Parent: I really hear you don't want to go to the doctor. Tell me why you don't want to be at the doctor. What don't you like about it? Is something scaring you about you being there?

Practice listening attentively to your child. Even be willing to share from your own childhood and what had you not wanting to go to the doctor. Resonate with your child's feelings and suggest ways to resolve their issues.

Having constant conversations with them gives a mutual connection and level of intimacy that allows the child to think deeply for himself. The child is then able to have time to think through what he or she may be dealing with.

A practice of having the child look within for the answers to any issue he or she may face, gives the child a strong reference point to always rely on.

Withholding Judgement and Criticism

I remember that I was so innocent that I was already 12 years old when I was told that the stork did not bring a child flying through the air to your house. However, what sticks in my mind is that somehow we must have believed that our children came from another world and are a gift to us.

At the beginning of the book, I mentioned that children come with batteries included. We must adhere to this truth as parents and respect the divine in our children as well as in ourselves. We are born with a true self. It is best described below:

> 'Dharma' is a Sanskrit word that has many varied meanings, depending on the context in which it is used. At its most expanded meaning, dharma is being true to one's essential Divine nature, while acting in the spirit of harmony and unity, knowing that all things and events are part of an indivisible

whole. Individually, everything has its own expression of its Divine origin and nature and has its own purpose, its own role to play, and its own responsibility in harmony with all.

In our early years, especially as babies, we are fully accepted as we are. We are the focus of our caregivers' lives. It is in this stage of development we can observe what I have termed as the "essential nature of the child." The baby "is" itself. It cries when it does, it sleeps when it does, it is calm when it is, etc. We are with our children at this stage. We are in acceptance of who they are, and while we want them to sleep all night, or eat on a regular basis, it is our concern for their well-being that is always at the forefront of our actions. I know many of us are already thinking about where our child will go to nursery school or some parents feel that their child needs a caregiver because they need to go to work. However, it is true that at this early stage we are more in acceptance than we are of our children when they are past 2 years of age.

Our parenting style cannot lose this connection and acceptance as our children become older. We must, of course, teach them the appropriate manners and ways of conducting themselves with others. This takes time and patience. It is really a full-time experience. Our gift to our children is to accept them as they are. This will allow them to be happy with who they are and in turn not be dependent on the approval of others. This can only be developed with a model of parenting that allows the child to have the right to make choices, have a right to his or her own thoughts and feelings, make mistakes, and learn to correct their own behavior at each stage of life.

Creating A Contract With Your Children

Here's a little tip that I have come up with:

After the age of 10, I suggest that a contract be created between parents and children where there is a negotiation process, and, in conversation, the child will make agreements and commitments and choose consequences. Then the contract is signed by the parents and the child. This contact gets revised as they grow into their teenage years or they leave the home.

Guidelines for Enforcing The Contract

There must not be nagging, lecturing, or preaching on the side of the parent. Support your children to keep their promises and commitments. It is natural for them to forget or not have the same amount of commitment as adults have. Therefore, be a reminder. For example, let's say they have agreed to feed the cat between 5 and 6 pm. You can say to your child, "I think the cat is hungry," or, "Do you think the cat is hungry?" These are reminders without attacking the character of the child. Make sure that you also acknowledge what each child does in keeping their agreements. This will reinforce their desire to please the parent. Another example: if the bed is not done in the morning, put a note on the bed that says: "You forgot to make me look nice this morning. Please don't forget to make me look nice," or, in the case of clothes on the floor, put a paper on the clothes that says, "I like to be put on hangers, please," or, "I don't like to be thrown here on the floor."

We want to preserve love and connection with our children. You want to always cut them some slack without violating the rule. Remember, rules are primarily to teach order and commitment. Rules are not to be turned into a way to create discord. Remember, we all forget sometimes, and children are daydreaming and changing before our eyes.

Everything a parent does with and for their children is a teaching tool.

Reflections

This way of parenting may sound very idealistic because it is outside of most people's experience, and certainly was outside of my own. It's a practice.

Raising our children and having the time, energy, patience, and unconditional love necessary is more than a full-time job. When we are single parents, working full time, or we are in relationships that are not working, it is certainly frustrating not only for the parent but also for

---

the children who often get less time, attention, and support. The parent is at their "wits end" not being able to nurture their own needs and well-being. It is certainly more than challenging.

Being Authentic With Your Children

We seem to believe that we have to keep reality away from our children. We tell them that children come from the stork or that Santa Claus brings them presents at Christmas or the bunny rabbit comes at Easter time. Did you ever ask yourself why? Don't we need to tell them the truth?

As I mentioned before, I know that we must protect our children. However, I suggest that we nurture their intuitive intelligence to become aware of what feels safe and unsafe for them.

First, be real with them. Practice honesty in the home. As a parent, be open and honest with your children. Let them know what is really occurring, not your interpretation. For example:

> *"Jane, daddy and mommy are not getting along because we argue and sometimes we just don't like each other. We are going to live in separate houses."*

To most children, of course, this would seem strange. Especially when we're telling our children to get along. Most children, unless there were devastating events in the home, would tell you to fix the problem. Yes, you will say, but we as a parent may be so devastated in our relationships that we don't know how to fix the problem. I say, get help! It's available to you and it is part of the journey of life. This is how we teach our children to be in the world. We show them that people see things differently, sometimes break their agreements, are out of integrity, lie, take advantage of each other, and that this does not work. Your children will already know inherently that this does not work. What seems monumental to us as adults is not monumental to our children. Unless you instill your fears and feelings onto them, children see things as events that occur in the moment. For example:

> *"Your dad fell in love with another woman other than me. He does not want to live with mommy anymore."*

This fact may make them feel sad because they want their parents together. Children are focused on how events threaten their safety. We are the ones that create the drama around the events which influence the safety, or lack of it, to our children. We must let our children know that, in the physical world, people will:

- Have differences of opinions

- Suffer great losses and learn to cope with them

- Die, and we don't know where they go

- Lie

- Do hurtful things and take advantage of others

- Want to be loved

First, we must be honest with our children and then coach them on how to deal with these events. At times they will feel angry, hurt, sad, empty, alone, etc. However, if we nurture and teach them how to cope and overcome any event, they will learn to face the challenges that life deals them and hold to their truth, even when others may disagree or exclude them.

Giving Your Children Choices From a Young Age

A s parents, we must always remember to grant them the space to create change in the world. This is done when our children are given a "voice". While the parents ultimately make the final decisions in their home, it is crucial that we listen to our children and have their feelings, points of view and ideas heard. By a voice I mean, that we grant them the space to speak and even have differences of opinions. All human beings need to be heard.

When our children are given the space to share their views it increases their ability for self reliance. Their power in life is to have self-determination. While I said before that they come with batteries included, we need to empower and assist them to activate these unique characteristics so that they can actualize effectively.

How Do We Do This?

At each stage of development, view your child with respect —they are a little person, not "just a child". Put yourself in their shoes while at the same time standing in your own role as an effective rational parent. While your children are continuously developing, remember that there is nothing missing in them. They are in a developmental stage. You must respect and trust your child as you parent them. When you have created this trust and respect, you develop the patience needed to give your child appropriate choices from an early age.

Example: a two-year-old can choose between two types of cookies, fruit, juices, toys, etc. At each stage keep giving them choices.

Entrusting Your Children to Collaborate

The authoritative model of parenting was focused on making our children into our likeness, or at least into our idealized likeness. We wanted these perfect little "robots" that would please us. This is not only unrealistic but very self-serving. It says to our children, "As long as you please me then I will give you my love. If you are not following the program that I believe in, I will take away my love."

We want to have collaborative children. How do we do this without breaking their will? My insights and experience have shown me that it is natural and important to set boundaries with everyone in our lives to preserve a sense of self. When we are raising children, we do not typically teach them to create their own boundaries. The authoritative method of parenting forces our will on them. We create many rules to control their behavior. We want them to do as we say, when and how we say without question. Rules are guidelines to create order and to make sure that we have mutual respect for one another. We tell our children who they should be, what we want from them, and what we expect, and, when they don't comply or live up to our expectations, we get angry and frustrated. We want them to be appropriate in the social structure we live in. We have used techniques such as corporal punishment, fear tactics, and the withdrawal of our love to break our children's will to get them to obey.

To teach collaboration, we must give them choices. Even if they are minimal choices to begin with, otherwise when they are older, we wonder, "Why doesn't she think for herself?"

Children are never asked what they need or want from the parent.

Managing Resistance in Your Children

The authoritative methods of parenting may have achieved obedience, but certainly not co-creation. With this method, we destroy a crucial ingredient to our creativity and uniqueness—our freedom of expression and our unique voice. We may achieve control, but we unknowingly bring about resentment in our children and cause them to have a splintered sense of self.

When I refer to a splintered sense of self, I mean that on one hand they may comply to appease the parents or others while what they think and feel is not expressed. When human beings stuff our feelings, we become less and less present.

Children are easier to control until they reach puberty. However, some strong-willed children are the ones we call "difficult children" because we cannot seem to break their will or get them to collaborate. What happens? We get into power struggles with them. We meet their resistance by using force to overpower their will.

Many parents may believe that when their children display resistance, they don't know how to deal with it, so they end up having a "battle of wills" with their children. This, of course, does not work. Why? Because, while in most cases children may be trying to assert their will; in my view, when a child or anyone demonstrates resistance, it may be a symptom of not feeling loved. What do you mean, you say? "I love my child." While we may love our child conceptually or intellectually or even deep in our hearts, we need to put action behind our love. Most of us don't know how because we are too programmed to fix things and not listen. We want to get something done and we struggle with the child's will to "get them" to comply. We must access love when we encounter differences with our children.

Resistance is a natural response to being told or led where we don't want to go. "Well," you might say, "you can't always do what you want to do. We need to teach our children that they cannot live a life of immediate gratification." This is true. However, it is the way that we teach this that will or will not bring about tremendous amounts of resistance. How? Here is the key.

When you are "love in action" you are not trying to manipulate nor control. You take every moment of being with your children as a gift and you are in full acceptance of the job that is before you, even when this job is challenging. This acceptance allows you to be fully involved in your role as a parent. You know that it takes time and patience and explanations, and you make sure that you make the time. From the time that they are able to speak, you tell them what you expect of them. You use appropriate language for their age, and you are well aware of what they are able to comprehend at each age. You respect their development, and you show them by giving them a "personal space" to make choices, even as early as two years old. When you give choices to your children, they begin to think for themselves what they want and don't want. They value their own point of view and this fosters self-confidence and self-reliance.

Example: You may decide that your child can choose between two or three cereals in the morning or between three storybooks at night. As they get older, you expand the list of choices.

I remember when I gave my son his choice of cereals in the morning. He had a selection of the small boxes of cereals. It was his choice to mix a few together and to play with the cereal before he ate it. Yes, it did take more time, so while I had to work, I made sure we had extra time. You see, what gets transmitted to your children is not only your love for them but your love to parent them. When they feel your love and the love to parent them, they don't need to start to resist you or your expectations. When you give them space to be part of the rules and guidelines they are not dictated to, they feel a part of you and the home. It is important also to have them contribute to the home. This makes them feel valued and gives them responsibility. You must not only model responsibility, but you must also teach responsibility by giving them room to contribute. You give room for your children to contribute when you view them as whole and valuable from the time they are born. Unfortunately, this is not always the case. We have a difficult time accepting that, but just because our children are a certain age does not mean that they are not insightful, intelligent, and wise. They are, and we must help them exercise these qualities. We do this by asking them questions or observing what they do if you ask them to do something that most people would not ask of a three-year-old.

Example: I remember being with James, my friend Bridget's four-year-old son. I knew that he was an insightful and sensitive child. How? I was very present with him and observed these qualities. I knew that he liked to feel strong and important. I would go over to their house, and I would play with him in what some would call an unusual way. I might say to him, "James, I am really hungry and a little cold. Can you get me something to eat?" First, he would go and get a baby blanket out of the crib and then he might bring me a cookie. I praised him, of course. I would also ask him questions about fish, which he liked a lot. I might ask him, "Do you think the fish are tired of being in the water?" He would answer me saying,

"They like the water." This type of interaction transmits to the child that they are valuable and that they can contribute, even when the parent is in charge.

I remember asking my son questions like, "What is the most important thing in life?" He would answer, "Love, mommy, or God." I remember always being amazed at the wisdom that he displayed and, later, the wisdom that all our children display. Unfortunately, most parents miss this incredible contribution to their lives because we are too busy just trying to get our children to fit in and do as we want them to.

Children resist when they don't feel heard or understood. We as parents need to communicate that we understand.

How To Engage Cooperation and Eliminate Resistance

Describe what you see: "I saw your bed was not made this morning."

Give information: "The bed looked like it was hit by a cyclone."

Say it with a word: "BOOM!!"

Talk about your feelings: "I was tired just looking at the bed."

Write a note: I like to look nice and neat.

Empowering Your Children to Listen to the Answers Within

How do you nurture this quality in your children? Remember that you are the model that your children learn from. If you take time out to commune with yourself, you naturally will give this to your children. You will have a way of being that reflects that you are a curious observer of life.

Example: When my son was just ten, he had to make a choice between two things that he really wanted to do. He was really worrying and having a rough time deciding what was the best choice for him. I asked him to close his eyes and to get really quiet. I had him breathe deeply and directed him to just let himself relax. I then said to him, "Imagine that there are no wrong answers and that whatever you choose right now is just perfect the way it is, what would you choose to do?" He took his time and then made his choice.

To this day when faced with a difficult decision, he tunes inward and trusts his answer.

Listening With The Heart

Developing your child's spiritual body empowers him or her to have high self-esteem and self-worth.

When you teach your child that there is a power within them that they can always tap into, and you guide your child to listen to their own inner guidance, you are giving them access to a source of power that is constant for them. It is a resource that inevitably will give them the possible solutions to whatever problem they may be challenged with when their parents are no longer there to help and support them, and it will help them to learn to rely on and to trust themself. In so doing, they can avoid getting caught up in what "the world's collective consciousness" is demanding of them. They will be more able to detach from peer pressure and feelings of needing to be liked or to be part of a group, especially in situations that may not genuinely be in their best interest.

Dealing With Your Children as they Reach Adolescence

C hildren rebel in their teenage years because they did not feel heard and acknowledged in their pre-teen years. Rebellion is an aspect of not being heard.

One of the problems that adolescents experience with their parents is that, when they are no longer totally dependent on their parents and are reaching for their own meaning of life, parents are not able to accept them. How parents have envisioned that their child "should be at this age" becomes the primary focus and, when the adolescent does not comply and shows resistance, parents' criticisms and frustrations grow and the relationship becomes alienated.

What the adolescent needs most is the safe space to work out their emotional growing pains. An "unsafe space" becomes created when parents don't have the room within themselves to tolerate or listen to or support the frustration and pain of dealing with issues that the young adult may be facing. How many times have I heard a teen say to the parents, "You tell me to be my own person; you have told me I should have my own ideas, but, when I demonstrate them to you, you just give me criticism or you dismiss me." The simple truth is that they need to be heard. When someone really hears what we feel, think, and want, it validates us. That is, it makes us whole. When we are in conflict, we feel internally fragmented. When someone is there to really hear us, even if they don't agree but they hear us out, we feel restored. This is the most important thing that our adolescent children need, as well as to feel trusted by their parents even when they make mistakes. 'Mistake' is a wonderful word because it really means that, like in the movies, they do many takes of a scene. Mistakes are just that. We tried something and we did not hit the desired mark. We didn't hit the bullseye and, sometimes, we didn't even hit the board. Nonetheless, we are still worthy. If our relationship with our children is respectful and loving, and there is a strong sense of trust, then we can hear them out and influence them to try other ways that may be more successful. However, if at each mistake we are angry and critical, our children will feel wounded and, as teens, they will close up and allow their peers to influence them. The parent's unconditional love will be the cradle that cushions and eases the challenges that growth produces.

Adolescents need you to listen to them.

A list of DON'Ts for parents:

Blame or accuse

Name-call

Threaten

Order or command

Lecture and moralise

Use martyrdom statements

Make comparisons

Speak with sarcasm

A list of DO's for parents:

Pay attention, no interruptions

Withhold any judgment

Take a few moments to reflect on what was said

Clarify anything you didn't hear or understand

Summarize what was said

Identify the moment you are in. "I am sitting here. I said I was going to read to my child."

Make being mindful a practice

Listen without intending to respond. Breathe when you are eager to respond or interrupt. Slow yourself down

Reduce distractions

Birth is a Miracle

Your child came to you as a miraculous gift of nature.
He or she was born through you and nature made no errors
and neither did you.

A fundamental point in finding joy in raising our children is not only to want them, but to be ready, willing, and able to love them. You see, when your heart is truly open and you are in wholehearted acceptance, the job of raising a child is never viewed as a struggle. You may have frustrating moments, but, because your love is so present, you just love doing whatever is needed for your child. Your love and being focused on the task are never in question. You love doing it. You would walk ten miles, stay awake for as long as it takes, whatever it may be, because you love your child, and you love the day-to-day experience of raising them.

When a child is born outside of what is seen as a normal child in the world we live in, the child is not stamped with delight and approval. I invite us to step outside of what our socialization process has granted us as what it is to be "normal". I suggest that normalcy is a myth created and carried over through time. At childbirth, we are sometimes anxiously awaiting the "perfect" child. This child looks right and has no health, mental or physical challenges. If the child does not bear these characteristics, we may feel disappointment, shame and often guilt.

I say, every child comes "as is." Every aspect of life is "just the way it is". We don't look at a bird and say, "it's a shame it doesn't have fur" or a dog "too bad it doesn't have feathers." Why? Because human beings compare and created a consensus of what "normal" looks like. If you as a parent or a child are not inside this consensus, you are odd, different, and not necessarily welcomed with love and acceptance. This creates a huge impact both on the parent and the child. They both start their lives together in an environment of trying to find a way to have the child be acceptable and accepted. All the while in the order of nature, not society, he or she enters the world as a precious gift.

I relate below the story of a courageous woman who was impacted by the myth of "normalcy" and finally has claimed the gift of her son's birth.

29 years ago Helen and her husband waited for the birth of their first born child. When Oliver was born, the joy and exuberance of being a mother drained out of her as the doctors took her newborn son from her arms for testing. When the doctors returned, they said: "He was born with a condition where his oesophagus is shaped like a test tube and the part coming from the stomach is joined to his lung. We have to rush him to another hospital for surgery." Helen held her son for only a few minutes before he was taken from her. She remembers leaving the hospital in a wheelchair with the celebratory balloons and flowers, but no child. This was the beginning of a long and very demanding journey of special care for Oliver during which Helen recalled trying extremely hard to "fix" him so she wasn't seen as a bad parent who would be unable to manage her child.

For years after his birth Helen dealt with Oliver's issues, including seizures, intellectual disabilities, destructive behaviors and the many ways Oliver showed his inability to cope with the world. He was very impulsive, and he quickly escalated to anger and rage - both physical and verbal. Despite repeated interventions, his ways of being were certainly not acceptable. She wanted him to be like other kids. She kept making play dates with children only to feel embarrassed when he yelled at or hit them. He didn't behave the way children "should." Even so, she kept hoping that one day Oliver would be "normal."

At age 10 he was diagnosed with a rare chromosome anomaly which explained his behavior but left Helen and her husband with no guidance as to how to support Oliver and their other two children. Helen was committed to finding answers as she was constantly dealing with Oliver attacking his siblings. The home became a battleground where she, her husband and the two other boys never knew what Oliver might do. Would he throw a book? Would he verbally scream and shout until he was exhausted? Or what? Sometimes Oliver would just turn and punch you for no reason. The impact was everyone was constantly vigilant, on edge and never sure when the next aggressive outburst would occur. The home was never safe.

Recently when Helen was reading a book about a woman who gave birth to a boy with Down's syndrome and described her joyous welcoming of her child, Helen began to weep uncontrollably. In that moment, the avalanche of tears gave way to letting go of years of holding back her pain and guilt. She began to be present to the gift and discovery of who Oliver is. Helen now delights in his straightforward way of communicating. He does not hide his feelings and he expresses what he likes and dislikes openly, mostly without aggression.

His way of being is refreshing in a world we live in where the quest for normalcy often has us live in pretense and denial. We live filled with fears and apprehension. We live in a world of getting it right. Oliver does not.

In one of our many incredible sessions, Helen's heart overflowed when she saw the preciousness of Oliver's life. The joy and magic, the awe and wonder that is in every single life! No matter what someone is born with - Down's syndrome, only three fingers or any condition that we may not consider fitting into the realm of "normal," she saw that each life is sacred as it is. Her son was to be honored, cherished, upheld and uplifted. Thirty years of challenges, difficulties, and heartaches with herself, her children and her life melted away. We looked at each other as tears rolled down from our eyes. Our hearts were fully open resonating in the radiant universal song of love for the sacredness of life.

My deep desire is that this book awakens your compassion and love for yourself as a human being, as a child and as a parent. That you spend quality time with your child and listen with your heart wide open to the gifts and lessons that your child brings to you. The future of our world is in our hands to nurture our children as we **Listen With Our Hearts**.

References

How To Talk So Kids Will Listen & Listen So Kids Will Talk

~ Adele Faber & Elaine Mazlish

Parenting from the Inside Out: How a Deeper Self-Understanding Can Help You Raise Children Who Thrive

~ Daniel J. Siegel, M.D. and Mary Hartzell, M.Ed.

Homecoming: Reclaiming and Healing Your Inner Child

~John Bradshaw

Inner Bonding: Becoming a Loving Adult to Your Inner Child

~ Margaret Paul, Ph.D.

Healing the Shame that Binds You

~John Bradshaw

The Spiritual Child: The New Science on Parenting for Health and Lifelong Thriving

~Lisa Miller, Ph.D.

The Secret Wisdom of Nature: Trees, Animals, and the Extraordinary Balance of All Living Things

~Peter Wohlleben

About The Author

Dee Martin, Founder of Inner Healing Through the Arts, The Creativity Encounter Program, The Gift and *Listening With The Heart*, has integrated her unique background and training as a Psychologist and psychotherapist with over 38 years experience to create a new Integrative Healing Method for personal and spiritual development. This method is a culmination of many years of personal exploration and study of diverse philosophical, theological and psychological disciplines.

Ms. Martin completed two years of undergraduate studies at the University of the City of New York (Baruch) and received her degree as a Licensed Clinical Psychologist at the John F. Kennedy University in Buenos Aires, Argentina. She has conducted private sessions, group sessions and seminars in both Spanish and English, as well as lectured in Argentina, New York City, Los Angeles, and Bermuda. Her education as a psychologist began in South America with studies in psychoanalysis and she expanded to include Transactional Analysis, Gestalt Therapy, Behavior Modification, Voice Dialogue, Rational Emotive Therapy, Inner Child disciplines as well as Analytical Psychology. She is also trained and experienced in Ontological Transformation as well as a variety of alternative therapies such as Reiki, Bioenergetics, reflexology. She currently, coaches individuals, couples and families in creating effective relationship dynamics.